Camping in
Comfort

Ragged Mountain Press / McGraw-Hill

CAMDEN, MAINE · NEW YORK · CHICAGO · SAN FRANCISCO · LISBON · LONDON
MADRID · MEXICO CITY · MILAN · NEW DELHI · SAN JUAN · SEOUL
SINGAPORE · SYDNEY · TORONTO

Camping in Comfort

· LYNN HANEY ·

A Guide to Roughing It
With Ease and Style

The McGraw·Hill Companies

1 2 3 4 5 6 7 8 9 10 DOC DOC 0 9 8

Library of Congress Cataloging-in-Publication Data
Haney, Lynn.
    Camping in comfort : a guide to roughing it with
ease and style / Lynn Haney.
        p. cm.
Includes index.
ISBN 978-0-07-145421-6 (pbk. : alk. paper)
1. Camping—Handbooks, manuals, etc.
2. Camping—Equipment and supplies.   I. Title.
GV191.7H36 2007
796.54—dc22
                                2007001048

ISBN 978-0-07-145421-6
MHID 0-07-145421-7

Questions regarding the content of this book should
be addressed to
Ragged Mountain Press
P.O. Box 220
Camden, ME 04843
www.raggedmountainpress.com

Questions regarding the ordering of this book should
be addressed to
The McGraw-Hill Companies
Customer Service Department
P.O. Box 547
Blacklick, OH 43004
Retail customers: 1-800-262-4729
Bookstores: 1-800-722-4726

Chapter opening photo credits: 1, 3, 4, 5, 7, The
Coleman Company, Inc.; 2, RVIA; 6, 9, Johnson
Outdoors, Inc.; 8, Aaron Teasdale/Adventure Cycling
Association; 10, Winnebago. Front Matter: pages i
and iii, The Coleman Company, Inc.; ii, Johnson
Outdoors, Inc.; vii, ix, Camelbak. Back Matter: 129,
Dahon; 132, 136, The Coleman Company, Inc.

Icons by Shannon Swanson

For Sarah and Alexander

Contents

Acknowledgments

Where to begin? First, I want to thank my husband John and our children Sarah and Alexander. Through sun, rain, hail, and high water, they proved to be intrepid and resourceful, offering suggestions, feedback, and spirited criticism.

Next, I'd like to offer collective thanks to the many friendly faces I encountered on trails and at campsites who willingly contributed valuable tips on equipment and pointers on comfortable camping spots. Similarly, I want to extend appreciation to generous friends who shared recollections of their outdoor adventures. I especially want to thank Judith Barbosa, a talented photographer who allowed me to create a campsite (more like a tent city) on her property to field test some of the gear.

There are dozens of equipment makers, designers, company representatives, publications, and organizations who are deserving of heartfelt thanks. Numerous individuals went out of their way to share their expertise, technical material, and photographs to make this guide as accurate and useful as possible. Among them: Simon Ashdown of Adventure Medical Kits, Jeff Basford of Paha Que, Jessie Bender of Aquapac, Michael Collin of Thule USA, Peter Devlin of the Outdoor Retailer show, Tami Fairweather of Therm-a-Rest, Mavis Fitzgerald of Ruff Wear, Clay Hardin of High Gear, John Hoge of Sea Eagle, Erin Keefe of Johnson Outdoors, Dax Kelm of CamelBak, John McDonald of ReserveAmerica, Mike May of Brunton, Mark Mallen of Camping Logic, Alli Noland of Buck Knives, Jordan Schultz of Crazy Creek, Emily Snayd of Merrell, Dave Teufel of L.L. Bean, Ben Therrien of Yakima, Aaron Teasdale of Adventure Cycling Association, and Ann Walden of Coleman.

In equal measure I would like to thank the employees at Trailblazer and North Cove Outfitters in Branford and Old Saybrook, Connecticut, respectively. Their advice on the purchase and maintenance of camping gear was indispensable. Special thanks to the remarkably knowledgeable staff at my local hangout, the Guilford Free Library.

Finally, I'd like to salute the consummate professionals at Ragged Mountain Press. Thanks to Jonathan Eaton and Tristram Coburn for greenlighting the project. I am particularly indebted to Bob Holtzman for coaxing this book into shape, ironing out the rough spots and providing expert guidance to ensure that it is a comprehensive and up-to-date resource on pleasurable camping. Also, I have benefited from the excellent editorial and technical advice of Ben McCanna, Julie Van Pelt, and Barbara Feller-Roth. Their astute suggestions, way with words, and technical knowledge have improved every chapter and I deeply appreciate their commitment to make this guide as accurate and useful as possible.

Kudos to Molly Mulhern and Janet Robbins for the imaginative design of the book and its cover. With good grace, forbearance, and attention to detail, they wrestled with an unwieldy number of photographs I sent their way.

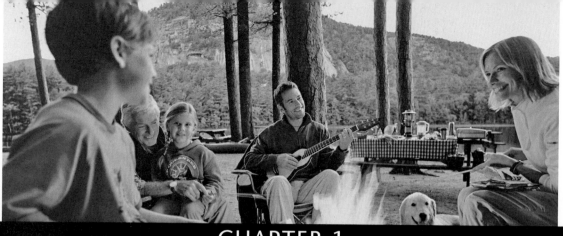

CHAPTER 1

MODERN CAMPING

One balmy summer night several years ago, while camping off the coast of Down East Maine, I sat on a log and twirled a hot dog over a crackling fire. My husband and two children joined me in this time-honored ritual.

I wondered: Can a vacation get any better than this? We had just spent a week hiking, kayaking, mountain biking, swimming, and lazily pitching stones over cool, clear waters. Now it was time to go home. "Where shall we camp next year?" I asked brightly.

"In a hotel," retorted my son. He popped a marshmallow into his mouth and glanced at his sister. She nodded in agreement. They had obviously discussed the matter.

How could such a shocking idea emanate from the lips of my own flesh and blood? Our annual pilgrimage to the great outdoors was a family tradition, our way of washing off the dreck of civilization.

As the number-one camping enthusiast in the family, I couldn't help but take the hotel suggestion personally. Had the kids gone soft? Did my children have issues with Mother Nature or—heaven forbid—their own mother?

"A hotel sounds great to me," chimed my husband. As he spoke, I noted he was leaning perilously forward on one of our dilapidated camping chairs. The plastic webbing had shredded away from the rickety frame. Collapse was imminent.

At his feet sat Quincy, our Labrador/golden retriever—a foundling from the streets of New Haven. The mutt of my dreams was fixing me with baleful eyes. What's going on? I asked myself. Dogs love camping.

"We're just fed up," my husband volunteered. "We come back to our campsite at night, and we're forced to reckon with this lousy equipment. It's time for a change."

As the evening wore on, the campfire stories revolved around our battles with the elements, and with our gear. "Remember when our tent blew away in the hurricane?" marveled our daughter.

"It was only a tropical storm," I corrected her.

"Well, my sleeping bag felt like a wet sandwich," groused our son. "And when I washed it at home and took it out of the machine, all the insulation had clumped to the bottom."

With a heavy heart I scanned the scene. Our threadbare tent was suspended from wobbly poles. Inside it stood four cots with their middles sagging, each cot topped by a thin pad. The gauntlet was thrown. I had to come up with a solution fast. Otherwise, camping *en famille* was history. And I regarded this piece of our lives as too valuable to toss away.

Love of the outdoors was bred into my bones. The offspring of a huntin' fishin' father, I grew up camping high in the Allegheny Mountains of western Pennsylvania. As a student in Paris, I backpacked through Europe on a few dollars a day, sleeping in haylofts, hostels, and the outbuildings of chateaus. Returning to the States, I pitched my tent at music festivals, political rallies, and on coastal beaches.

But it wasn't just for my own sake that I wanted to safeguard our family's camping experience. The values of camping were something I wanted to pass on to my children. I wanted to instill in them the sense of unpredictable adventure that comes when you exit the beaten path. And camping was a way to help them see the country's natural resources up close and convey the importance of preserving them for future generations.

But their complaints had merit. Like many families, we had purchased our gear willy-nilly at big-box retailers. We hadn't given much thought to quality or durability. So it was not surprising that our equipment had not held up well.

The next morning as we wended down Maine's Route 1 and I puzzled over our meltdown, I had what I call "my epiphany." If we could avail ourselves of the latest technological innovations in camping equipment, we could make our outdoor experiences almost hassle-free. As if by divine intervention, we approached a sign for L.L. Bean: gear nirvana. "Pull over!" I barked at my husband.

Anyone who ventures into one of America's great gear emporiums is immediately struck by how camping has taken on a bright new look. The venerable old brown boots and drab-looking tents in subdued hues have been replaced by cheerful colors.

Much of the new gear is user-friendly, compact, durable, and downright stylish. It gives nature lovers the freedom to enjoy the outdoors without being hamstrung by cumbersome, weighty equipment.

These gear headquarters are vacation destinations in themselves. Companies rent space in their cathedral-size rooms for conferences, and couples have even been married in these stores (guests are surrounded by gift ideas). Much of the stores' popularity has to do with a resurgence in outdoor pursuits. Camping is the number-one outdoor vacation activity. According to a recreation executive report, one-third of the adults in the United States has gone on a camping vacation in the last five years. Since 9/11, camping activities have risen 30 percent.

Increasingly, Americans are choosing to bring home amenities to their campsites. "We still have diehards, folks who want to rough it and take the minimalist approach," says Jim Reid, an executive at Coleman, "but the much, much stronger trend is families who want to maximize convenience and comfort."

Returning home from Maine, I donated any salvageable gear we owned to Goodwill; the rest I tossed in the dump. Then I set about mastering camping in the twenty-first century. During the process, I enlisted the help of experts in outdoor equipment, field-tested products and sought honest opinions from other campers.

I soon realized that outdoor enthusiasts want the straight scoop. You're hungry for accurate information about gear—particularly new merchandise that's lightweight, portable, and practical. You may be put off by the mind-boggling lingo of technical gear and wonder whether some of this gear is reserved for the outdoor elite. You want specific tips on how to cut through the feature-intensive confusion and simplify your needs. Most of all, you don't want to be burdened with advertising hype and hearsay.

What's the best way to tackle this book? You can read it straight through, or you can zero in on your particular interests. The chapters cover gear, activities, and modes of camping. Let's be clear, however: This is not a primer on the basics of camping, nor is it a handbook on the fundamentals of particular outdoor activities, such as "How to Backpack" or "How to Kayak and Canoe." Numerous books have already tackled these subjects. What's more, this book isn't written for campers who are interested in strenuous or highly technical pursuits such as through-hiking, mountaineering, whitewater paddling, or transcontinental bike touring. And it has little to say to no-pain no-gain purists who regard endured hardships as badges of honor. Rather, this book is written specifically for fun lovers who simply want to enjoy nature with minimum hassle and maximum pleasure.

CAMPING CHOICES

So what exactly is camping in comfort? For some, getting back to nature means a campground bustling with RVs and barbecues. For others, it is a string of wilderness days away from the maddening crowds. For many, it is somewhere in between—a park, a riverbank, or a sequestered cabin.

Car Camping

If you are car camping at a state park, for example, your site can become a virtual outdoor suite with multiple tents, inflatable mattresses, collapsible tables and chairs, and sturdy kitchen equipment such as a portable range and a barbecue grill.

Many developed campgrounds offer restrooms with hot showers, laundry facilities, picnic tables, tent platforms, trash cans, and electric outlets at the tent sites. Some campgrounds even schedule organized activities for children (to the relief of many parents).

Car camping is more comfy than ever with multi-room tents, portable rugged tables, and folding armchairs. (The Coleman Company, Inc.)

FAMILY CAMPS

If you'd like to undertake a variety of camping activities with your kids but don't want the bother of packing and planning, you might explore the increasingly popular option of family camps. Family camps are similar to resorts but they're a bit more rustic. Many traditional children's summer camps offer family camping on designated weeks or weekends.

The family camp experience offers parents the best of both worlds: time to spend with their kids, and time to spend away from their kids. Children's activities for all ages up to eighteen ensure parents a couple of hours of downtime every day.

See Appendix C for a list of family camps.

Backpacking

If backpacking is on your agenda, welcome to weight watchers. If your assembled gear is too heavy to move, perhaps you'd better stay home. Backpacking—particularly ultralight backpacking, which has revolutionized the sport—is an exercise in relentlessly minimizing weight in order to be comfortable. To reduce what you carry, you might search out titanium tent poles, LED (light-emitting diode) flashlights, and sleeping bags that fold to pocket size.

Not so long ago, backpacking tents were little more than crude shelters. Now, with the advent

A comfortable pack has adequate strap/support systems and weighs less than five pounds empty. When packing, evenly distribute the volume and weight. (Johnson Outdoors, Inc.)

of superlight, waterproof, ripstop fabric, you can have a luxurious tent that weighs a mere two or three pounds. Today's packing tents are well built, rugged, easy to store, and simple to set up.

Minimalism for backpackers also extends to clothing. A wind shirt, for example, allows you dress in lighter base layers during active exercise in cold conditions. Footwear, too, is lighter. There is a saying that "a pound on the foot equals five pounds in your pack." For this reason, many people have moved away from full-blown boots and now hike in low-topped hiking shoes.

Boat Camping

Compared to backpacking, canoe camping and kayak camping are outdoor luxuries. Boats can easily transport you, your family, and all of your gear across the lake to your favorite campsite in the woods. Think of these boats as floating pieces of luggage.

See Chapter 9 for more on boat camping.

Bicycle Camping

Bicycle camping brings other joys and challenges to creating a comfortable campsite. Like backpacking, biking is noteworthy for its self-sufficiency. Bike campers, however, can carry more gear.

If you are a cyclist making overnight stops, camping in comfort means being well equipped for the demands of your particular sport. You'll want to carry tools and spare tubes and tires. Lack of preparation in this case could mean you'll spend a night camping on the roadside.

Like backpackers and kayakers, cyclists are focused on weight. They can pack more volume than a backpacker but not as much as a boat camper. Biking with a heavy load in panniers or a

Kayaks and canoes can carry all your equipment and are easy to paddle and haul ashore. They give you access to island campsites as well as pristine mainland beaches and secluded bays unreachable by road. (The Coleman Company, Inc.)

COMPARISON OF DIFFERENT TYPES OF CAMPING

MAXIMUM WEIGHT OF GEAR PER PERSON IN POUNDS (APPROX.)	MAXIMUM VOLUME OF GEAR PER PERSON IN CUBIC INCHES (APPROX.)	ACCOMMODATIONS	COOKING GEAR	PROS	CONS
BACKPACKING					
45	3,600–4,000	Small tent, sleeping bag, pad	One-burner stove/small cook kit	Closest to nature Most access to remote areas Most self-reliant	Slowest mode Must carry everything Minimalist equipment/ less comfort
BICYCLE CAMPING					
60	5,000	Small tent, sleeping bag, pad	One-burner stove/small cook kit	More distance covered than backpacking Gear transported on bike, can carry more than backpacking Good views of scenery	Less access to remote areas than backpacking
CANOE/KAYAK CAMPING					
400 (canoe) 150 (kayak)	8,000 (canoe) 6,000 (kayak)	Large tent, sleeping bag, pad or air mattress	Two-burner stove/ medium-sized cook kit	Access to boat-in-only campsites Larger gear capacity than backpacking, biking	More vulnerable to changing weather conditions on and around water Equipment must be waterproof
CAR/TRUCK CAMPING					
500	8,500	Large tent, sleeping bag, pad, air mattress, or cot	Two- or three-burner stove Wood or charcoal grill	Can cover a lot of ground, see more country	Limited to drive-in sites

COMPARISON OF DIFFERENT TYPES OF CAMPING (*continued*)

MAXIMUM WEIGHT OF GEAR PER PERSON IN POUNDS (APPROX.)	MAXIMUM VOLUME OF GEAR PER PERSON IN CUBIC INCHES (APPROX.)	ACCOMMODATIONS	COOKING GEAR	PROS	CONS
RV CAMPING					
Thousand of pounds	Tens of thousand of cubic inches	Bed with the vehicle—total weather protection	Electric or propane stovetop/conventional or convection oven, microwave	Homelike amenities	Least contact with nature Less maneuverability than car or truck Often limited to perimeter campsites Adds to air and noise pollution Most expensive

Living off your bike in the great outdoors can be a comfortable experience. Bike campers are able to carry a little more gear than backpackers, although some of the extra weight will be tools and spares for the bike itself. (Jeff Hiles/Adventure Cycling Association)

trailer, even on flat, well-paved stretches, is a lot more strenuous than day biking. For minimalists, tents are available as small as a pound and a half for one person and three pounds for two people. For the more comfort conscious, an extra tarp ensures protection from cold, wet ground, although it adds a pound of weight.

Well-equipped camping cyclists also give special attention to their clothing and equipment. Safety gear is of particular concern to bikers.

See Chapter 8 for more on bicycle camping.

RV Camping

At the far end of the camping spectrum is RV camping. RV owners carry their living quarters with them. They have comfortable beds with innerspring mattresses. Showers. Closets. Couches for lounging and tables for dining and playing games. A clean bathroom that's always nearby. What else could you want? Well, toys are nice—specifically ones that fit into the confines of your rolling cottage.

Recreational vehicles allow you to camp with all the comforts of home. (RVIA)

That's why inflatable boats that pack down small, and lightweight bikes that fold up, are so popular with RV vacationers. These campers also appreciate traveling with their laptops, entertainment systems, and plenty of food to cook in the built-in microwave.

See Chapter 10 for more on RV camping.

Cabins

My favorite way to camp in comfort is to hole up in a solid structure, say in a cabin, yurt, or tree house. Click on www.reserveamerica.com, a government-contracted reservation service, and you'll discover a world of options. More than fifteen hundred public-use cabins pepper the nation's state and federal lands. Some are rustic tent cabins; others are more like a home away from home. Full-service cabins offer queen-size beds, private bathrooms, electricity, kitchen utensils, and outdoor grilling areas. The park system also lets you rent decommissioned fire lookouts atop Colorado peaks, surplus forest-guard stations along Rocky Mountain rivers, and Mongolian-style yurts facing the Pacific. Yurt camping is

Tent cabins allow you to experience the pleasures of the outdoors in a comfortable environment. Some include modern conveniences, such as electricity and heat. (Sweetwater Bungalows)

on the rise and is also available at many private campgrounds.

Luxury Camping

For those who think the call of the wild should be answered by room service, we'll even take a look at luxury camping. Glamorous camping, or *glamping*, is growing steadily both in the United States and abroad. The idea is to cultivate an atmosphere as nice as a hotel but retain the sights and sounds of camping. Think of the cushy amenities provided by safari camping outfitters on the Serengeti. You'll learn about places such as El Capitan Canyon Campground in Santa Barbara, California, where for $285 a night you can chill out in an elegant

Designer tents at luxury camping resorts offer down comforters, wet bars, solar-powered Internet access, and handcrafted willow beds. (El Capitan)

canvas tent with a handcrafted willow bed, linen service, maid service, and massages.

Flashpacking

Like luxury camping, flashpacking is also on the rise among outdoor travelers. These campers like to take to the woods with accoutrements such as digital cameras, cell phones, laptops, battery chargers, batteries, power adapters, and flash cards (hence the name *flash*packing). The proliferation of internet wireless is abetting this trend.

■

GETTING THE GEAR

This sourcebook is by no means the last word on all the equipment that's out there. There's simply too much of it. Instead, consider this book a starting point and a navigating device to steer you through the vast array of gear available, and as a means of streamlining the selection process.

But lacking the latest gear shouldn't keep you from camping. Equipment is easy to find and can be as simple or as elaborate as you like. All you need are a few basic items, such as a tent with rainfly, sleeping bags, sleeping pads, flashlight and/or lantern, cookstove, mess kit or individual place settings, matches, and—very important—a good first-aid kit.

You can also cast a wide net with friends and relatives to see what you can borrow. Or rent gear from a local outfitter; most rental places have all the items available, from tents and sleeping bags to lanterns, cook stoves, and utensils. And don't forget the secondhand market, virtual as well as real-world (check out sites such as geartrade.com, ebay.com, and craigslist.com).

Just keep in mind that function is the key to happy camping. So don't cut corners on quality. Unreliable equipment can ruin a camping trip as quickly as foul weather. This doesn't mean you have to take out a home equity loan to outfit yourself for the great outdoors. With the checklists, shopping tips, and websites listed in this book, you'll be able to take advantage of the many bargains available.

Whatever kind of camper you are, durable equipment that you enjoy is a central part of creating a pleasurable outdoor experience. A little up-front research can prevent hours of frustration at the campsite and on the trail. If you outfit yourself with the appropriate gear—then plan your trip, prepare well, and pack carefully—you are ensuring a successful camping experience.

CHAPTER 2

SAFETY AND FIRST AID

Now that you've had a taste of modern camping, are you ready to give it a try? Perhaps you're hesitating because you fear a camping trip could result in broken bones, poison-ivy rashes, snake bites, or water-borne illnesses. Take heart; a few moments of education and preparation can help ensure your health and safety.

Most minor camping setbacks are no different from what you might encounter in your backyard: your husband trips on a downed branch and sprains his ankle; your daughter puts her hand on the hot barbecue grill; you get overzealous carving a watermelon and take a small chunk out of your thumb. If you can handle any of these problems at home, you can handle them while camping, too, as long as you are prepared.

FIRST-AID KITS

Educate yourself in basic first aid and bring a well-stocked first-aid kit. Be prepared to treat cuts and scrapes, bee stings, or allergic reactions. (If you plan to venture into deep wilderness, miles from the nearest ER, consider taking a first-aid course with an organization such as the Red Cross.) Even if you haven't taken a first-aid course, many prepackaged kits include a first-aid book with step-by-step instructions to help you manage minor injuries.

If you choose to assemble your own kit, consider the following basic items:

- ▶ *exam gloves*
- ▶ *sharp knife/scalpel*
- ▶ *tweezers*
- ▶ *scissors*
- ▶ *iodine*
- ▶ *self-stick bandages*
- ▶ *gauze*
- ▶ *waterproof medical tape*
- ▶ *blister pads*
- ▶ *topical antibiotic*
- ▶ *anti-diarrheal pills*
- ▶ *pain relivers*
- ▶ *antihistamine pills and cream*
- ▶ *EpiPen*

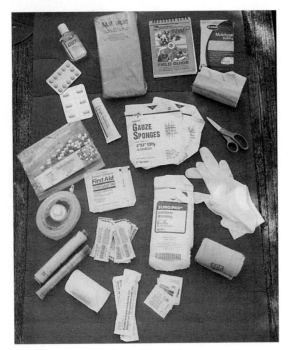

First-aid kit. (Annie Aggens)

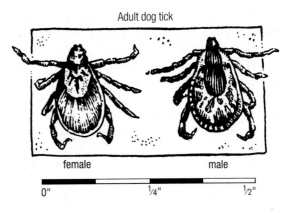

Adult dog tick

female   male

0"   ¼"   ½"

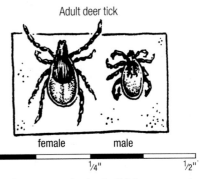

Adult deer tick

female   male

0"   ¼"   ½"

Check for ticks on a regular basis. While most are harmless (e.g., dog ticks), some ticks can transmit diseases to people and animals (e.g., deer ticks). (Christopher Hoyt)

Other safety items include maps, a compass, flashlight, pocketknife, waterproof fire starter, personal shelter, whistle, warm clothing, high-energy food, water, and insect protection.

INSECTS

Creepy crawlies are probably the biggest threat to camping comfort. Be prepared to face mosquitoes, ticks, flies, blackflies, deerflies, redbugs, hornets, yellow jackets, and wasps.

Far from being just an itchy annoyance, mosquitoes are disease carriers. In recent years, West Nile Virus has become a problem in North America. Thankfully, the chances of contracting West Nile Virus are very slim, according to the Centers for Disease Control. For the most part, mosquitoes are just a nuisance, but take precaution and use bug spray.

Ticks are disease carriers, too; namely, Lyme Disease. If you're camping in tick country, inspect your family every night and have someone inspect you. Inspections are particularly important if you've been walking in tall grass. Ticks like to hide on scalps, behind ears, in armpits, and in the groin area. Regularly check pets, too.

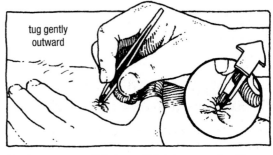

tug gently
outward

The best way to dislodge a tick is to grasp it with tweezers as close to the skin as possible, and tug gently outward. (Christopher Hoyt)

If you find a tick, remove it. Using tweezers, grasp the tick as close to the skin as possible. Do not grab the tick in the middle part of its body. Ticks may carry harmful bacteria, and squeezing their abdomen may inject the bacteria into the wound. Once you have a firm grasp of the tick, pull it straight out. It's likely that the tick's mouthparts will break off during the removal process and remain under the skin. If so, should you dig them out? There are two competing opinions on this. On the one hand, the embedded mouthparts can cause a secondary infection, and should be removed like a splinter. On the other hand, you might do more harm by digging out the mouthparts with a needle, and the mouthparts will eventually slough off anyway. To avoid this dilemma altogether, carry special tick tweezers that are designed to remove the tick completely.

Contrary to popular belief, you should not smother the tick with Vaseline or burn it. These methods are not effective in removing the tick and may force infected fluid into the bloodstream.

Most importantly, don't panic if you find a tick. Not all ticks are infected with Lyme disease. Besides, studies have shown that infected ticks don't begin transmitting the disease until thirty-six to forty-eight hours after attachment.

A bee sting can cause a serious medical emergency. If any member of your party is allergic to bee stings, make sure you carry an EpiPen in your first-aid kit.

WILD ANIMALS

Aside from insects, other creatures big and small can sabotage our comfort. We go camping to commune with nature, but what happens if nature decides to commune with us? A close encounter of the furry kind isn't always comfortable. Wild creatures have their own agendas, and their desires can play havoc with our food, our gear, and possibly our lives.

So how can we be safe and at ease on their turf? The answer is to mind your manners, treat creatures with respect (that means not stressing or harassing them), familiarize yourself with their habits, and take the necessary precautions to prevent campsite raids.

Bears

Bears strike fear in the hearts of campers like no other animal. Fortunately, bear attacks are exceedingly rare. Encounters with bears, however, are on the rise.

Bears are generally shy, solitary animals, but they're becoming increasingly desensitized to humans. This is partly due to shrinking habitat, but campers are also to blame. There's an old saying: "When a pine needle drops in the forest, a turkey sees it, a deer hears it, and a bear smells it." A bear's sense of smell is highly attuned, and the lure of easily available food in a crowded campground can quickly overcome a bear's natural timidity. In heavily used regions like the Sierra and Blue Ridge mountains, and in most of our national parks, bears can seem as commonplace as squirrels.

Proper planning is the key to avoiding problems in bear country. Proper food storage, in particular, is crucial. A bear-proof canister is the ideal method of food storage. Seal your food in the canister, then place it on the ground at least 100 yards away from camp. A bear will take a keen interest in the canister, but it will eventually move on once it realizes the canister is impenetrable.

Some campsites provide steel food lockers called *bear boxes*. If a bear box is available, you *must* use it.

If bear boxes aren't provided and you don't have a bear-proof canister, place all your food in a nylon camp bag and hang it from a tree. The bag should hang at least 10 feet from the ground and at least four feet from the tree trunk.

Don't pitch your tent just anywhere. Keep sleeping areas away from bear boxes and cooking areas. If

Some wilderness campgrounds provide stationary bear boxes to store extra food and anything that has a scent (toothpaste, sunscreen, baby wipes, and cologne). (National Park Service).

possible, pitch your tent upwind from the cooking area. Also avoid setting up camp next to a roaring stream. Bears that hear you, will usually avoid you.

Also carry the phone numbers of local authorities (park rangers, sheriff, etc.). Report any incident involving bears.

A final thought. Animals in the wild have just as much right to comfort as you do. If you aren't careful, your intrusion into their space may disrupt

their mating or nesting or interfere with their feeding. So as you venture into the woods and mountains, pay attention to wildlife's well-being as well as your own. Remember, you are guests in *their* home.

DEHYDRATION

Dehydration is a significant safety issue. Water is essential for nearly every bodily function, including digestion, respiration, brain activity, and regulation of body temperature, and it is also important for comfort. Dehydration occurs when a person loses more fluids than he or she takes in. It isn't as serious a problem for adults as it is for babies or young children. Look for these signs of dehydration: thirst, dry mouth, dark urine, irritability, fatigue, rapid pulse, pale and sweaty skin, nausea, swollen tongue, slurred speech, impaired vision. For a mild case of dehydration, drink water until your urine turns clear and symptoms disappear. Get to a hospital immediately if your symptoms don't abate; severe dehydration is deadly.

Portable secure canisters are a lightweight and effective way to protect your food in bear country. (Chris Townsend)

Chemical treatment with iodine (left) or chlorine (right) is an inexpensive option for water purification. (Chris Townsend)

Pump filters are another option for purifying water. (Chris Townsend)

The MIOX purifier (developed in conjunction with the U.S. military) is ultralight, easy to use, and can purify enough water for large groups. It needs only camera batteries and salt to operate. The MIOX works best on water with no sediment or debris, so it helps to rid the water of solids with a paper coffee filter before adding the MIOX solution. (Chris Townsend)

The SteriPEN is a water purifier that disinfects with ultraviolet (UV) light to destroy waterborne microbes. Operating on four alkaline AA batteries, it purifies 16 ounces of water in a minute and a half. It should be used only on clear water; sediment hinders its effectiveness. (SteriPEN)

For better-tasting water, you'll need to get a water filter or a water purifier.

WATER-BORNE ILLNESSES

It can be tempting to drink water straight from a babbling spring, but don't. Microbes and other nasties can be found in even the clearest water. Treat all water from natural sources.

Iodine caplets are the easiest, cheapest solution. You can buy these caplets in almost any camping-supplies store for five dollars or less. Drop a few tablets in a quart of water, wait twenty minutes, and you're good to go. The taste of iodine-treated water, however, is not great.

LIGHTNING

Lightning is another frightening prospect for many campers, especially boaters who can't easily retreat to a car. Although more people are killed by lightning than by any other weather phenomenon, it's unlikely you'll ever be struck. Still, it's a good idea to improve your odds even further.

16

When an electrical storm approaches, seek shelter immediately. If possible, take cover in a building or your car. Tents offer no protection from lighting, and tents with metal frames can be downright hazardous. Lying down inside a tent is particularly dangerous because ground currents can run through you from head to foot. Seek alternative shelter if possible.

Mountain summits and exposed ridges are extremely hazardous during lightning storms. If a storm develops, quickly descend the mountain away from the direction of the approaching storm. (Mountain thunderstorms tend to form in the early to mid-afternoon. For this reason, it's best to hike the high peaks in the early morning.)

If, during a lightning storm, your hair stands on end, skin tingles, or you hear crackling noises, then a nearby lightning strike is imminent. Quickly assume the *lightning safe position*: crouch down with your feet together, center your weight on the balls of your feet, lower your head, and cover your ears.

HYPOTHERMIA

Most campers understand that hypothermia is a danger during cold weather, but it also can occur when temperatures are well above freezing. Cases of hypothermia occur can happen during any season. Always dress appropriately and stay dry (see Chapter 6). Food and water also help your body maintain energy levels and stay warm.

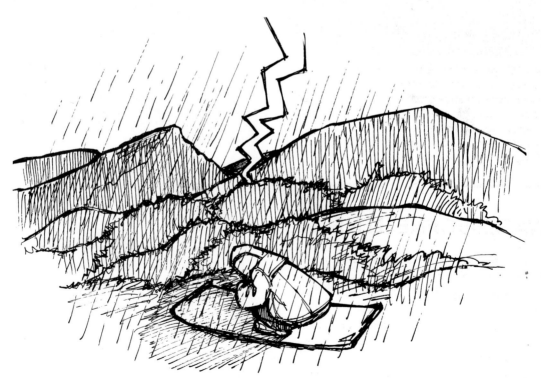

Crouching will lessen your chances of getting hit when lightning strikes. Squat down and wrap your hands around your legs. Close your eyes and keep your feet together. (Christopher Hoyt)

GETTING LOST, OR STAYING FOUND

Daniel Boone said he had never been lost, but he admitted to being "mighty confused for several days in a row." Getting lost happens to the best of us, so plan ahead carefully and follow commonsense safety precautions.

For starters, carry a reliable map and compass. Neither is expensive. Second—and this should be obvious—learn basic map and compass skills (and teach them to your children) before you venture into the outdoors. Get a book on wilderness navigation and practice the techniques at home. Basic navigation can be mastered in an afternoon.

If a map and compass seems dreadfully old fashioned, consider a GPS receiver. GPS equipment is now widely available and surprisingly affordable. Keep in mind, however, that GPS receivers are not foolproof. Batteries die and gadgets break. In many ways, there's simply no substitute for a paper map.

Compass skills are essential for outdoor navigation and safety. (Johnson Outdoors, Inc.)

A GPS receiver makes it easy to navigate, but pack a backup map in case your batteries run out. (Garmin)

CHAPTER 3

TENTS

Tent quality can make or break a camping trip. You won't realize this on an exquisite summer night when the sky is clear and the air is balmy. But as Dave Barry says, "Rainstorms will travel thousands of miles, against prevailing winds, for the opportunity to rain on a tent." And it's when a nasty rain pelts the roof of your nylon shelter and a fierce wind threatens to flatten it that you'll know whether your tent is made of the right stuff.

ASSESSING YOUR NEEDS

Your tent is your most important piece of camping equipment. It must protect you from water, wind, and insects. A failure to do any of these is not only uncomfortable, it's potentially dangerous. A tent should also give you a sense of privacy and security once you're zipped inside for the night.

A tent is also one of the most fun pieces of gear to purchase. Still, for neophytes, the experience can be daunting. There are many choices of color, size, and style—from high-tech models used by alpinists to multi-room cabin tents made for fair-weather family camping. There are three-season tents, four-season tents, dome tents, tunnels, free-standing tents, tents with vestibules, biking tents, hiking tents. The list goes on.

No type of tent is inherently better than the others, but there are varying degrees of quality within each group.

Primary Use

If you're planning a backpacking or a bike camping trip, tent size and weight become primary concerns. Almost any lightweight tent can be used for these activities. Also, shorter pole sections minimize the length of the packed tent. An ultralight nylon tunnel tent would be a good choice, because it can be rolled into a tight bundle the size of a football.

On the other hand, if you and your family are planning on a one- or two-week stay at a campsite, a cabin tent (up to 20 feet in length) is a good idea.

Most cabin tents have separate rooms, allowing for privacy. Some have large vinyl windows, which help eliminate the claustrophobic feelings you might otherwise experience when rain keeps you inside. Cabin tents take a long time to set up and break down, so they're not a good choice for short-term camping.

Lightweight backpacking tents and cabin tents represent the extremes at either end; you'll find many options in between to meet your particular style of camping.

Number of People

Determine how many people will be using the tent and the sleeping space desired for each person. Also, consider how much headroom you will want inside the tent. Will you be spending much time inside? Most campers like some elbow room.

The rule of thumb for camping in comfort dictates that your tent should provide at least 15 square feet per person.

Next, give some thought to what kind of sleeping gear you will have inside the tent. In addition to sleeping bags, will you have air mattresses, mats, or cots? Contemplate the numbers and sizes of each and what other equipment will be stored inside.

Family camping usually requires a large multi-person tent. In this situation, important attributes are spaciousness, breathability (loosely woven fabric permits breezes to penetrate a tent, resulting in greater comfort), and perhaps separate compartments for privacy.

Consider modular tents—shelters that can be freestanding or linked together with zippers. Another popular solution for large groups or families is to buy several tents—one for parents and another for children, or one for males and another for females.

Camping Season

Do you camp only in summer, or are you a four-season camper? Do you expect sun, rain, or snow in whatever season you choose? Ventilation is important for summer camping, whereas winter camping requires a tent that's impermeable to wind and foul weather. If most of your camping will be done in summer, you won't need to spend the extra money for a four-season tent. You can bring along a tent heater for the occasional cold night.

Modular tents can be connected to one another or used separately. (Bibler Tents)

It's always fair weather in a tent if you've got a propane catalytic heater. (The Coleman Company, Inc.)

Cost

You get what you pay for. More expensive tents usually have stronger fabric, poles, and stitching than lower-priced tents. This means they can withstand higher winds and heavier rain. And they will last longer. But not all campers need a tent that is extremely strong and durable. An expedition tent might win a best gear award but it's overkill if you're spending a weekend at a luxury beach campground.

A family of frequent campers will need to seek out the most durable tent they can afford, whereas a recreational camper may choose a suitable moderately priced tent.

■

TYPES OF TENTS

Three- or Four-Season?

Within all the various style groups, tents can generally be divided into two basic types: three-season and four-season tents. Three-season tents are ideal for general use in good to moderate weather conditions. For most campers, three-season tents offer the best combination of comfort features, weight, price, and protection. While three-season tents can withstand rain, wind, and insects, they also provide excellent ventilation on a hot summer night. Thoughtful design elements include fast and easy setup, convenient storage, windows and skylights in some, and a vestibule for added space (for muddy hiking boots, wet gear, et cetera).

Four-season tents are built to handle more severe weather and are usually used during winter skiing, hiking, and mountaineering trips. Expedition tents, a type of four-season tent, are designed to withstand high winds, heavy snow, intense exposure to ultraviolet light, and driving rain. For most campers, an expedition tent would be overkill.

Three-/four-season convertible tents are four-season tents that can be modified to suit warmer weather. This type of tent is an excellent choice for hikers who expect to experience a wide range of climates during their hikes. When camping in the summer months, several tent parts can be left at home to minimize weight. For instance, when pitching the tent in three-season mode, some poles are optional. The tent will be less sturdy, but a lighter pack is a fair trade off. Besides, most convertibles feature internal-guy systems and numerous

Expedition tents are designed to provide safety and comfort in the harshest conditions. Their great strength and ruggedness comes at the price of weight and cost, however, and may be overkill for most campers. (Johnson Outdoors, Inc.)

Convertible tents offer maximum versatility. They are designed like four-season tents (left) but can be converted to three-season tents if the added protection isn't needed. (Johnson Outdoors, Inc.)

external guy-out loops, allowing you to stiffen things up considerably during windy conditions.

Now let's take a look at all the different types of tents.

Dome Tents

The aerodynamic shape of a dome tent allows it to shed wind and rain more effectively than other styles. Perhaps for these reasons alone, the dome is the most popular tent used today. Despite what the name implies, dome tents rarely have a circular footprint. Dome tents come in a number of shapes, including rectangles, hexagons, or octagons. Domes range in size from single-person to twelve-person tents.

Dome tents are easy to set up. In most cases you expand collapsible poles into long, flexible rods. Next, you thread the rods thread through sleeves in the tent fabric. When you bend the rods into position, the dome forms and, voila, you have

A basic dome tent is the best choice for many backpackers and bike and boat campers. Dome tents are lightweight, easy to set up, and stable. (Johnson Outdoors, Inc.)

a freestanding tent. A freestanding tent doesn't require stakes or lines to stay up; the rods do all the work. This is a valuable feature for rocky areas where stakes are out of the question.

A freestanding dome tent has other advantages, too. Provided it's empty, you can lift and move a fully erected tent to, say, a shady spot, then return it to its original location at bedtime. And if you want rid the tent of sand or leaves, simply remove your gear, then lift the tent and shake the dirt out the front door.

Keep in mind, however, that stakes are generally included with freestanding tents and they should be used whenever possible. If your tent hasn't been properly staked, a strong wind can send an unoccupied tent rolling through the campground like tumbleweed.

The drawback of domes is that the sloping sides of the dome mean you'll hunch over a lot. Even large tents that have standing room under the center of the dome, won't have much useable airspace elsewhere.

Another disadvantage of domes is that moisture tends to gather at the top of the dome, where it condenses and drips on sleeping campers below.

Setting up a dome tent takes eight to twelve minutes; it's generally a one-person task.

Cabin Tents

Cabin tents were once the staple of the classic family vacation. These homes away from home provide plenty of room for cots, chairs, coolers, or even a large table. The spacious, square design means a high ceiling and nearly vertical walls. The average footprint of a cabin tent is 9 by 12 feet, but they're available in sizes that can accommodate twelve people.

Cabin tents are ideal in situations when weight is not an issue.

Cabin tents are a good choice if you and your family want to stay in one place for any length of time. It takes fifteen to thirty minutes to set up a cabin tent, and the task usually requires two or more people. With their straight walls and generous headroom, cabin tents provide more airspace than dome tents. If you're stuck in a tent during a protracted rainstorm, the extra room of a cabin tent may stave off cabin fever.

Tunnel Tents

Tunnel tents, also called hoop tents, are designed for weight-conscious backpackers and cyclists. These tents have fewer poles than domes, which reduces weight. Tunnel tents have a low profile that easily sheds wind and precipitation. Most are half-cylinders: curved sidewalls that incorporate three arched frame stays. Sizes range from one-person tents with very limited headroom to eight- or ten-person tents with headroom exceeding six feet.

Some tunnel tents feature a ceiling flap that, when folded back, allows you to peer at the nighttime sky through panels of mosquito netting.

Cabin tents are a good choice for campers who plan to stay put for a while. (Johnson Outdoors, Inc.)

COMFORT COMPARISON OF TENT TYPES

SIZE (sq ft)	HEADROOM (ft)	WEIGHT (lbs)	CONSIDERATIONS	BEST USE
CABIN				

Largest	High (7–12)	Heaviest (40–80)	Requires staking
			More difficult to
			  set up than domes
			Better ventilation
			  than domes
			High winds can be
			  a problem
				Car camping
				Campground use
				Camping with
				  groups/family

DOME				
Wide range (5.4–150)	Medium (3–6.5)	Wide range, but usually lighter in weight than equivalent size frame tent (4–30)	More resistant to high winds Not as much headroom as cabin tent Easy to set up	Car camping Backpacking Bike camping
TUNNEL				

Smallest
(10–37)
	Low (2–5)	Light (3–12)	Requires tethering in
			  windy conditions, even
			  with freestanding tents
			Can be as strong as domes
			Requires fewer poles;
			  lighter and more compact
			  when packed
			Some models designed
			  for extreme weather
			Fast and easy to pitch
				Backpacking
				Bike camping

Tunnel tents are among the most lightweight choices for their size. They are available in a wide range of designs, including ultralight models for solo backpackers, rugged expedition models, and ten-man tents with standing headroom. (Bibler Tents)

Ultralight tents generally weigh less than three pounds, a tempting option when weight is an issue. (L.L. Bean)

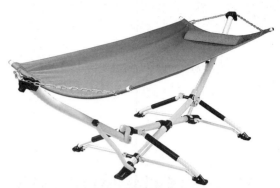

A camping hammock keeps you off the ground, away from rocks and tree roots. (The Coleman Company, Inc.)

One drawback of tunnel tents is that they are not freestanding; they require staking. Still, their shape is highly efficient for both weight and floor space.

Ultralight Tents

Ultralight is the current buzzword among backpackers and climbers who want to travel light and fast (or just light). Ultralight tents can be tunnel or dome designs; some can accommodate three people. Unlike conventional tents, ultralights have single-wall construction and they lack rainflys. Ultralights also have lighter-weight poles and stakes than their bulkier counterparts. How light is ultralight? The Eureka Spitfire UL, for example, weighs just over two pounds.

Other Tents and Shelters

Camping Hammocks and Tent Cots

Fun and cheap, camping hammocks and tent cots can be a comfortable alternative to a tent, particularly at a rocky or muddy campsite. Many camping hammocks and tent cots come with bug screens and rainflys. If you're hanging a hammock, make sure your anchor points are secure (avoid

dead trees). (For peace of mind, however, you might choose a portable freestanding camping hammock.)

Truck Tents

Truck tents add new meaning to the phrase "truck bed." These tents fit in the bed of a pickup truck. They're roughly 8 feet high and 7 feet long and they have large mesh windows. Truck tents allow you to sleep off the ground (far above any pooling rainwater), and they require no additional space at a campsite. If bad knees make it difficult to clamber in and out of the truck bed, bring along a set of portable stairs.

A tent cot provides self-contained off-the-ground comfort. (Kamp Rite)

A truck tent turns a pickup truck into a mini-RV. (Enel Company)

Inflatable Tents

Tired of fiddling with tent poles as the sun goes down? An inflatable tent may be a good option for you. Innovative air-poles replace rigid poles to create a structure that is strong and durable, yet fully collapsible. Some models are erected with a foot pump while others come with an air compressor that plugs into a car's cigarette lighter. Inflatable tents are available in 2-, 3-, 4-, and 6-person models.

Freedom Tent

Freedom Tent by Eureka! represents a breakthrough for campers with disabilities. Designed specifically for people who have special needs, the tent has zippers with big loops that are easy to grab and easy to pull. There's room for a private toilet,

Inflatable tents get support from airtight tubes rather than poles. (Nemo Tents)

The Freedom Tent from Eureka! is a luxury tent designed to be set up and used by people with disabilities. (Johnson Outdoors, Inc.)

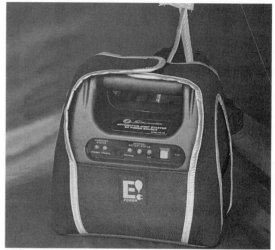

Eureka's N!ergy tent (left) looks like a normal tent, but the power pack (right) enables campers to use electrical appliances such as lights, a fan, or a mattress pump. (Johnson Outdoors, Inc.)

and its wide, no-lip entryway can accommodate a wheelchair.

Wired Tents

Let there be light—or fans, laptops, DVD players, cell phones, and other small electric devices. A new electrified tent from Eureka incorporates a portable, rechargeable battery, into the tent. The tent comes wired with three factory-installed 12-volt outlets that power the tent for camping comfort. Any 12-volt direct-current (DC) accessory can now be used while camping. Simply plug it in and turn it on.

TENT SIZE

Camping tents are sized by the number of people they can accommodate; two-person tents, four-person

---

ASK AN EXPERT

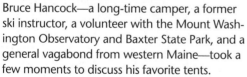

Bruce Hancock—a long-time camper, a former ski instructor, a volunteer with the Mount Washington Observatory and Baxter State Park, and a general vagabond from western Maine—took a few moments to discuss his favorite tents.

I have 2 favorite tents. For car camping—and especially for early season, heavy bug camping—the L.L. Bean King Pine Dome is excellent. I call it the camping condo because it has a built-in screened front porch. Sitting in a blackfly-free zone during June in Maine is a treat. For backpacking, canoe camping, or bike camping, the 1-person MSR Hubba and 2-person Hubba Hubba get my vote. They have vertical side walls, which increase the feeling of interior space. They also have a vestibule by the entryway where you can keep your wet or dirty boots out of the tent and also out of the elements.

tents, six-person tents, and so on. The manufacturer's claim, however, warrants skepticism. Generally speaking, a tent's size describes the maximum number of average-sized persons who can be crammed together. These sizes do not take personal gear into account either. To put it another way, you can cram twenty college students into a VW bug, but that doesn't make it a twenty-person vehicle.

Let's take a reality check: one-person tents are just *barely* big enough for one person; two-person tents are usually comfortable for just one person; three-person tents are comfortable for two people; and so on. Per-person ratings aren't consistent across manufacturers, either. If possible, go to a camping outfitter that has fully erected tents on display and take a "test drive." Crawl inside a display tent and lie down. Bring some friends. Is the tent as big as its manufacturer claims?

VENTILATION

To keep occupants dry, a tent needs to be more dynamic than a sealed plastic bag. Aside from the fact that you'd suffocate, a tent that doesn't allow for ventilation will retain moisture from its inhabitants. Each person exhales up to a full pint of moisture each night, plus a bit more in the form of perspiration. If you don't vent that moisture to the outside, it will condense on the inside of the tent (especially in humid or cold weather), run down the top and sides and drip in your face.

Tent designers deal with the ventilation challenge in two ways. The most common solution is the double-wall tent, in which the sides and top of the tent body are made of breathable ripstop nylon and mesh screens. Over the tent body is the rainfly, usually another layer of ripstop nylon that has been coated with a waterproofing agent. Inside moisture can exit the tent through the inner wall, while outside moisture is blocked by the rainfly.

The rainfly should cover the entire tent, but there must be enough room between the tent and the rainfly for air to circulate and disperse the exhaled moisture.

Don't be alarmed if some sections of the inner walls are wet after a cold or humid night, particularly at locations where the tent walls come in contact with the rainfly.

Ultralight tents, on the other hand, typically have only a single wall of waterproof material and no rainfly. Designers try to work in all kinds of vents, air scoops, and covered awnings on ultralight tents to help evacuate moisture. Although these measures are mostly successful, single-wall

Double-wall tents have mesh walls on the tent body (left) for ventilation, and a full-coverage fly (right) to keep out the rain. (Johnson Outdoors, Inc.)

Colder, damper, and less durable than a double-wall tent, a single-wall tent is best in low humidity and dry climates. (Johnson Outdoors, Inc.)

tents are inevitably damper than double-wall designs.

DESIGN FEATURES

Doors, Windows, and Ventilation

Heat creates the need for airflow, particularly on hot summer nights. Plus, after being outside for a couple of days, you and your roomies will be a tad, shall we say, "hygienically challenged." A well-ventilated tent is key to comfort.

The number and configuration of windows and doors can make a big difference in how easy it is to stay in a tent. Multiple doors enhance your comfort considerably by allowing for quick entrances and exits and eliminating the need to climb over your tent mates if you need to visit the facilities in the middle of the night.

Screens and Screen Rooms

All modern tents have mesh-screen netting over the windows and doors to keep insects out. Although the standard mosquito netting is made of nylon, higher-quality tents often use a finer mesh made of Dacron. This no-see-um netting keeps out those tiny gnats rarely noticed until they start biting. To a comfort lover like me, screens made of no-see-um mesh are of utmost importance.

If bugs are a possibility where you camp, a cabin tent with an attached screen room is ideal. You get protection from the flying beasts without sitting in a hot tent. A separate screen room is

Ventilation, provided by multiple screened windows and doors, is a key factor in tent comfort. (L.L. Bean)

even better, because it allows breezes to blow through from all directions. You can also set up a screen room over your picnic table for bug-free meals.

To keep the nasty critters out of your tent, remember to keep the screens closed except when you're entering or exiting the tent.

Room Dividers

A tent with room dividers allows you to break up space so you can relegate sleeping quarters to one section of the tent and gear to another. Available only in larger tents, these sheets of fabric hang inside the tent and can be zipped down to make a curtain-like wall or rolled and tied up to make one large room. With children, a two-room tent is ideal because the kids can go to bed early while the adults stay up. On the downside, dividers can keep you from using floor space effectively and hinder cross ventilation.

Vestibules

A vestibule is your tent's mudroom—an enclosed area without a floor that attaches to the front door of the tent. It's the perfect place to store wet boots, backpacks, or other gear that could get the tent floor dirty or take up sleeping space. Vestibules are either sewn on or pole supported. A pole-supported vestibule is heavier but is usually larger and more stormproof than one that is sewn on. Vestibules are often constructed as a modular accessory that you can leave at home when you don't want to carry the weight. However, a sewn-on vestibule has another advantage: Water has a harder time finding its way into your tent.

Gear Storage

Tent pockets—little pouches made of ripstop nylon or window mesh that are sewn to the inside of the tent—are indispensable for holding eyeglasses, keys, flashlights, or other small objects. Gear lofts—net slings that stretch from one side of the tent ceiling to the other—are an efficient use of

A gear loft, a mesh platform that hangs near the ceiling inside the tent, provides out-of-the-way storage—something that's in short supply in many tents. (Johnson Outdoors, Inc.)

space and are less prone to condensation moisture than pockets in the tent wall.

CONSTRUCTION FEATURES

Fabric and Color

Polyester fabrics are heavier than nylon, but they withstand exposure to ultraviolet rays better and, if the added weight isn't an issue, they're the best choice for long-term use. (One way to protect your tent fabric is to buy a UV protection called Fabric Guard 303. It costs about ten dollars per 16-ounce can at camping and marine supply stores. A single container should cover a small dome tent; three or four cans should be sufficient for a large dome or a cabin tent.)

The color of a tent affects the light levels inside the tent and the temperature. A light-colored tent such as beige, white, or yellow will be brighter inside and tend to reflect the sun's heat. A darker tent such as blue, green, black, or red will absorb more heat during daylight hours and also block more light from the interior.

Ease of Set Up

When shopping for a tent, give serious consideration to set-up times. This is particularly important if you will be camping alone. Ask yourself the following questions: How many stakes are required? How many poles? Must they be inserted under tension? How many guylines? What about the rainfly? How much separate rigging does it require? Could I set up the tent with cold hands, in the dark?

If you will be pitching a tent alone, look for a small tent with color-coded clips and color-coded poles for easier assembly. Some tents have glow-in-the-dark zipper pulls and reflective guy-outs, which are a big help for nighttime assembly.

Pole Attachments

There are two main ways to attach the poles to the tent body: clips and sleeves. Clips make for quick setup but they aren't as strong as sleeves. A clip can snap off—during set up or during heavy winds.

Sleeves, on the other hand, apply even stress across the length of the tent body, so they are less likely to rip during set up or in heavy winds. It can

Continuous pole sleeves are easy and fast, because you don't have to thread poles through multiple sections the way you do with smaller sleeves. (Johnson Outdoors, Inc.)

be difficult, however, to thread the poles through the sleeves, especially when wearing gloves.

Floor Construction

Tent floors should be made of tougher material than the lightweight sides and top. "Bathtub floors," which wrap a few inches up the sides, are the norm in quality tents. These keep the long and leak-prone side-to-bottom seam off the ground. Still, it's a good idea to buy a ground cloth if it's not already included in your tent package. The cloth will help protect the tent's bottom against punctures and tears from rocks and sticks, and will provide another layer between you and the wet ground. Some manufacturers offer ground cloths custom-fitted to their tents. If you want to save some money and still have a custom-fitted ground sheet, cut up an old shower curtain or a piece of heavy-duty polyethylene sheeting from a hardware store.

Zippers

Strong zippers are another important feature. They should open and close freely, and should not catch and bind up on the tent fabric. As mentioned earlier, some tents have glow-in-the-dark zipper pulls, which are a big help for nighttime bathroom trips. Zippers with double storm flaps keep the water out. Noiseless zipper pulls—found in high-end tents such as Sierra Designs and Kelty—are lighter than standard zippers and allow quiet, uninterrupted nights.

Seams

Poorly made seams are susceptible to rips and leaks. Seams should be sewn with many small, regularly spaced stitches. Seams on higher-quality tents are reinforced with a strip of cloth tape. Seams must be sealed with a waterproof seam sealer. Most manufacturers apply this for you but; if not, you'll have to do this work yourself. Many tent packages include a bottle of seam sealer regardless of whether the seams were factory-sealed. And, even if the factory did apply the sealer, many campers reapply it for added peace of mind. Set up the tent in the yard before your trip, and apply the sealer. Let it dry before packing the tent. You will need to do this yearly.

CHOOSING A GOOD TENT SITE

Much of the success of a camping trip depends on the campsite you choose. As your select your campsite, consider your daily needs. In a busy campground, look for a site a little off the beaten path. Trees, bushes, and some terrain features can screen your site from trails and neighboring campsites.

In an established campground, the layout of the sites is complete, and the basic amenities of a picnic table, fire ring, water source, and bathroom facilities are provided. Before you commit to a site, however, make sure it isn't next to noisy neighbors with a humming generator, a boom box, and rambunctious children. And stay upwind of the outhouse.

If you are backpacking, your first choice should be a pre-existing tent site. Whenever possible, you should avoid trampling vegetation. In all cases, study the terrain. Avoid camping in low-lying areas; higher ground is preferable. Avoid digging ditches around your tent; they leave lasting scars on the ground. From the perspective of environmental impact, the best kind of surface to camp on is bare ground and rock, but the most comfortable surface is forest duff (decaying leaves). If possible, choose an area open to the east and south that will catch sunlight early in the day. These areas may also stay drier than slopes facing north.

Take wind into account. If you're in in sheltered woods, wind is not a big issue. But if you're camping on a windy mountain top, you'll need to position your tent such that the end that has the lowest profile faces the wind. Always securely stake the tent and rainfly, even if it the weather is calm when you set up the tent.

TENT MAINTENANCE
Stay Clean and Organized

Who likes a dirty campground or a messy campsite? With a little effort, you can maintain order, have fun, and leave the campsite in good shape for the next person who uses it. Here are some suggestions:

▶ *Remove boots or shoes before entering the tent.*
▶ *Place a piece of carpeting at the doorway to catch debris. Pine needles and the like can create pinholes that allow moisture to enter. Some tents include doormats fused to the tent floor.*
▶ *Use a whisk broom and dustpan daily to keep the floor free from debris and small stones, which can abrade the bottom of the tent.*
▶ *Avoid keeping food inside the tent. Hungry critters will chew through the tent fabric in search of food.*
▶ *Keep your gear organized in plastic bins, packing cubes, duffels, or totes. Car trunk organizers made by companies such as Yakima, Thule, and Mountainsmith work well in a tent as well as a*

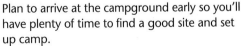

QUICK TIP: FIRST THINGS FIRST

Plan to arrive at the campground early so you'll have plenty of time to find a good site and set up camp.

Even if you arrive at the campsite hours before bedtime, setting up camp should be your top priority. If bad weather rolls in unexpectedly, you'll be glad your shelter is standing and not bundled up in a few bags. Plus, you'll enjoy your other activities more if you don't have work hanging over your head.

The Camping Closet fits snugly against the side of a tent and helps keep gear organized. (L.L. Bean)

vehicle. *The Camping Closet, made by L.L. Bean, my favorite way to organize a tent, is designed with multiple small cubbyholes that provide readily accessible niches for your small gear.*

Repacking

Whenever possible, let your tent dry in the sun before you take it down. If time or weather are conspiring against you, and you have to pack a wet tent, stuff it loosely in a sack and set it up as soon as you get home, or hang it on a clothesline and dry it completely

before putting it away. If you are backpacking, consider securing your tent on the outside of your pack and letting it dry while you hike.

A wet tent invites mildew. Mildew penetrates the urethane coating of the tent fabric and grows between the fabric and the coating, eventually causing the coating to lift. Thus the fabric is no longer waterproof and is essentially useless.

Cleaning and Storing

Yes, it's a pain, but you should clean your tent after each camping trip. At minimum, give it a thorough cleaning at the end of the season.

▶ *Hand-wash with cold water using a mild, non-detergent soap (such as Ivory liquid) and a nonabrasive sponge. Avoid scouring pads and abrasive cleansers.*
▶ *Rinse thoroughly and let air dry. (Avoid using a washing machine or dryer; they can damage the tent's protective coating and seams.)*
▶ *Clean the tent poles with a soft, dry cloth. (It is especially important to remove salt spray after oceanside camping trips.)*
▶ *Look for any debris trapped in zipper teeth, and remove it with a soft bristle brush. I use McNett's Zip Care to lubricate tent zipper teeth to reduce wear.*

Patching Holes

Eventually, you'll puncture your tent. Patching a tent is similar to patching an inner tube. Tent

BACKYARD CAMPING

Preparing your kids for the great outdoors begins in the backyard.

When our son Alexander was ten, we set up a large cabin tent, a wading pool, and camping chairs on our postage-sized lawn. The "campground" was such a success we left it up for the entire summer.

Children love waving good-bye as they disappear into their tent, relishing the freedom of being outdoors yet with the peace of mind of being right at home. These pleasant associations will serve them well when you take them on their first real trip.

patching kits are available, with fabric cement and patches of waterproof material. An air mattress repair kit will also work.

FINAL WORD ON CHEAP TENTS

Take it from one who's been there, a poor-quality tent will disappoint you. It will wear out quickly, develop problems such as broken zippers and split seams, and possibly leave you up a creek when the weather turns nasty.

I once set up a discount tent on the beach, and a pole snapped under the lightest stress. Then, wriggling into my sleeping bag for the night, I realized that the tent's flimsy netting wasn't up to the fierce insects who were eyeing me for their dinner. To make matters worse, a thunderstorm blew in during the wee hours. Rainwater pooled on the roof and seeped through the entrance.

If you compare a cheap tent to a good one, you'll see that the quality tent has better ripstop nylon or polyester and stronger aluminum poles, uses more stitches per seam-sealed inch, and has coated bathtub floors and no-see-um mesh netting.

So don't spend your money foolishly. Get a quality tent—one that makes your heart beat a little faster. Have technical requirements on hand when you go shopping, but don't underestimate your emotional response. A tent should grab you. My dad (a diehard romantic) followed this dictum when he went looking for a cabin tent for our family of six. He found a large green canvas shelter at the army navy store, and we christened it "Big Bertha." In time, Bertha showed her age and sprouted holes, which Dad dutifully mended. She wasn't high-tech or sexy, and she weighed a ton, but Bertha was Dad's dream tent—strong and unbending. Best of all, she helped create enduring memories. I recall lying on my cot on warm summer nights listening to the gentle patter of raindrops on canvas. For that magical sound, the newer nylon tents can't even come close.

CHAPTER 4

SLEEPING BAGS AND PADS

For as long as I can remember, I've kept a sleeping bag tucked in my closet. It's my magic carpet. When the urge to escape hits me, I know I can pack up my bag and set off in search of adventure. Romantic notions aside, past experiences have heightened my awareness of the fundamental purpose of the sleeping bag. To wit: it should be warm, dry, and roomy enough so you don't feel claustrophobic. It should fit you, be easy to pack, and suit the climate. In other words, it should be comfortable.

SLEEPING BAG RATINGS

Most sleeping bags are rated in two ways: by season and by temperature, or "comfort rating." If you're like me and do a lot of camping, you need at least two bags: one for warm-weather camping and another for cold-weather excursions.

Summer Bags

Summer bags are mainly for warm-weather camping and are good for 30 degrees Fahrenheit or above. These bags are mostly a rectangular or barrel shape (shapes are discussed later on). They're often designed for extra comfort: summer is the time to luxuriate in lots of room and linings that feel good against bare skin. Summer bags often have a full-length zipper that opens at both ends to maximize ventilation or even allow the bag to be opened up completely and used like a comforter.

Three-Season Bags

Three-season bags are for spring, summer, and fall. They are good for 10 degrees Fahrenheit and above. Due to their versatility, these are the most common sleeping bags on the market. They incorporate all three shapes of bags: rectangular, barrel, and mummy. If you want to purchase one bag to work for all three seasons, buy a bag with a temperature rating of at least 10 degrees Fahrenheit. This will

A NOTE ON TEMPERATURE RATINGS

The sleeping bag temperature or comfort rating identifies the coldest temperature the bag is designed to accommodate. For instance, a +20 bag is designed to keep you comfortable if the air temperature drops no lower than 20 degrees Fahrenheit. Naturally, *comfort* is a subjective term, so the ratings vary from manufacturer to manufacturer. Use these ratings as a guide, not a guarantee.

Also note that the ratings assume you'll be using a sleeping pad in conjunction with the bag. (We'll discuss sleeping pads in detail later.)

keep you warm on cold days, but won't make you sweat on hot summer nights.

Cold-Weather/Winter Bags

Cold-weather bags are usually rated to –10 degrees Fahrenheit. Snug is the way to go, because the closer the fit, the warmer you will sleep. For this reason, a mummy bag is preferable to a rectangular bag.

Extreme Bags

Extreme bags are designed to keep you warm at –40 degrees to –10 degrees Fahrenheit. These bags are exclusively mummy style. Extreme bags can also come with an extreme price tag. The lower the temperature rating, the more the bag will cost.

SHAPES

All of the sleeping bag designs currently on the market can be classified into three general types: rectangular; semi-rectangular, or *barrel*; and mummy. A bag's shape is important because it affects heat retention.

Rectangular

This is the most simple and still most popular bag. It's just the ticket for summer camping when you're

If you like to sprawl out and move your legs, consider a rectangular bag. (Johnson Outdoors, Inc.)

traveling by car or truck. Usually economically priced, a rectangular bag is like a super-duty quilt folded in half and secured by a big zipper. (It can be unzipped for use as a comforter, or two bags can be zipped together.)

Though they aren't as pricey as other designs, rectangular bags can be very durable. My uncle Rory (6 feet 4 inches and built like a lumberjack) prizes his monstrous, canvas-shelled, flannel-lined rectangular bag that he takes deer hunting in Wisconsin. He spreads it out on an oversize cot in the four-walled outfitter tent he shares with his buddies. The extra space of the rectangular bag offers him plenty of leg and shoulder room for his restless sleeping habits, but it's not very efficient. Rectangular bags allow more heat to escape than other bag styles. Their full rectangular shape means that more material is used in their construction, resulting in a bulkier bag that doesn't compress as well as other styles.

Semi-Rectangular, or Barrel

These bags offer a good compromise between space and weight. The rectangular shape is tapered slightly at the foot to help decrease overall size and weight. The barrel shape is slightly more compactable than a full rectangular shape. Semi-rectangular/ barrel bags are usually better quality than purely rectangular bags and offer a tapered opening and foot section, which help reduce heat loss. The design does not restrict the sleeper, allowing for more room to maneuver. These bags often come with special features such as hoods, collars, draft tubes (an inner flap that covers the zipper to provide insulation), and better-quality filler.

Mummy

Mummy bags are the warmest. Resembling an ancient Egyptian sarcophagus, they closely conform

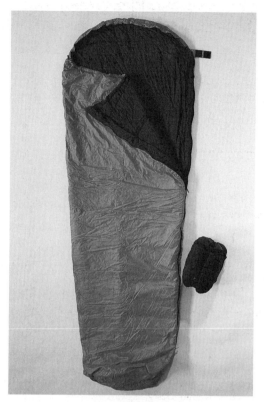

A compromise between a mummy and a rectangular design, a barrel bag is usually tapered at the bottom and some at the shoulders to reduce weight and bulk. (Cocoon by Design Salt)

to your body's contours—including your head—which means you won't waste energy heating unused air space. If you're a restless sleeper, however, mummy bags are not so comfortable. Their restrictive shape makes it difficult to toss and turn.

QUICK TIP: LET THERE BE LIGHT

Bring a flashlight for each person old enough to handle one. Flashlights are indispensable when nature calls in the middle of the night. Advise the children to use the flashlights only when necessary, but bring along extra batteries just in case someone plays shadow puppets in the tent into the wee hours.

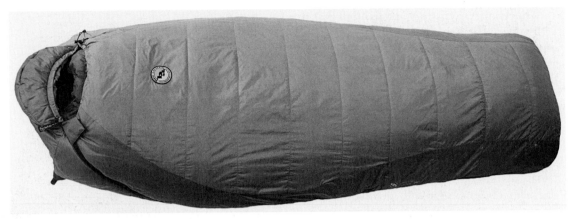

Mummy style sleeping bags are comfy in cold weather, but they're also confining. (Big Agnes)

Mummy bags are generally made with the highest-quality fabrics and insulations. They are lightweight and highly compactable, making them ideal for backpacking.

SIZES

It's important to make sure a sleeping bag fits your build. Bags come in two basic sizes: regular or long. Regular bags are usually made to fit a smaller person; a long bag is constructed for a taller person. If you are six feet tall or less, choose a regular length bag. If you are taller than six feet you'll need a long bag.

Bags also come in various widths, too. Sleeping bags are usually sized as follows:

▶ *Kids: 28 inches by 57 inches, smaller overall for less area to warm*
▶ *Junior: 29 inches by 66 inches, either a shorter bag or a slimmer bag for young adults or a petite person*
▶ *Standard: 33 inches by 75 inches, for the average-size person*
▶ *Oversize: 33 inches by 78 inches, extra long*

for a taller person; or 38 inches by 81 inches for a bigger person (or someone who likes more room)

NICHE BAGS

Getting the correct fit is not just a matter of size. The major manufacturers have done a good job of tailoring sleeping bags to suit everyone.

Women's Bags

Women are usually shorter (their average height is 5 feet 4 inches) and wider than men, and sleep colder, thanks to a slower metabolism. Women's bags typically have narrower shoulders, wider hips, and up to 20 percent more insulation than a man's bag with the same temperature rating. Many women's bags come in a short size—5 feet 6 inches.

Children's Bags

When buying for a child, you might not want to invest a lot in a bag that will soon be outgrown. So consider purchasing a larger bag that your child can grow into. You can tie off the bottom of a bag to

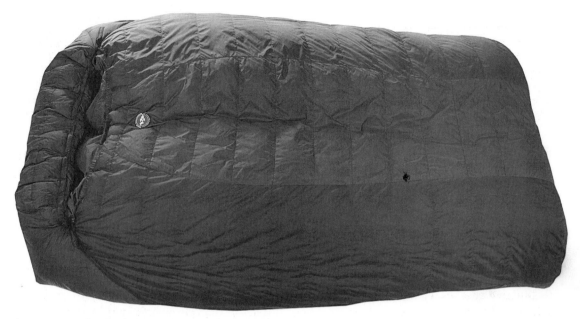

A two-person sleeping bag is ideal for the romantically inclined. (Big Agnes)

shorten it temporarily, or you can stuff the foot of the bag with clothing to increase its insulating value.

Another option is a modular sleeping bag. Modular bags are designed to grow with your child. For example, the Growing Bear, by Tough Traveler, can cover a growing child from four years old to seven (approximately). The bag starts at a height of 3 feet, but an attachable top extends the bag to 4 feet 10 inches. A smaller bag—The Baby Bear—covers 3- to 5-year-old toddlers.

Keep in mind that children's sleeping bags often get very dirty, so choose one with synthetic filling for easy washing. Also look for bags with oversized, kid-friendly zippers.

Double Bags

Some couples prefer to zip their bags together. If this option is important to you, make sure you buy bags from the same manufacturer. Also, make sure that one bag has a right-hand zipper and the other a left-hand zipper.

If separate yet compatible bags still seem too non-committal, you can opt for a two-person bag.

These double bags feature a zipper on either side which allows either camper to slip out for a bathroom break without disturbing the other. Plus, with two zippers, you can still use the bag if one zipper breaks.

Ultralight Bags

One-pound, ultralight sleeping bags are a boon to backpackers. Ultralight bags weigh as little as 17 ounces and can be stuffed into a bread bag.

You may be wondering, why doesn't everybody buy the lightest bag available? Simple: price. Ultralight bags generally cost $200–$300.

CONSTRUCTION

Every sleeping bag has a shell, a liner, and the insulation sandwiched between. The insulation, without a doubt, is the most important factor in choosing a sleeping bag.

Down Insulation

Down is the fluffy undercoating found just beneath the outer feathers of geese and ducks. This natural material provides more insulation per ounce than any other material.

Not all down bags are equal, however. Different bags contain different amounts of down. How can you tell the difference? Bags are rated by *fill power*—a measurement that refers to the loft, or fluffiness, of insulation per pound. If two down bags are similarly sized, the higher fill weight indicates a better insulation value. A bag with 600 fill power is fine, but a bag with 900 fill power is the pinnacle of quality. Low-grade 500 fill power sleeping bags are commonly found in department stores. These bags are fine for sleepovers at the house, but using them for camping is a recipe for a long, cold night.

Down bags are as much as 35 percent lighter than their synthetic counterparts. A down bag is also more compressible, so it will take up less space in your pack. Down is built for the long haul: it doesn't break down as fast as synthetics. This means a down bag will last three to four times as long as a synthetic bag. With higher quality comes higher price; down bags are almost always more expensive than similarly rated synthetic bags.

Aside from price, down's only disadvantage is evident when it's wet. A wet down bag loses virtually all of its insulating capacity, and it takes a long time to dry out. Many newer down bags have water-resistant shells that make down bags less vulnerable than they were in the past. But if your style of camping might expose your bag to a dunking, synthetic fill might be a better choice.

Synthetic Insulation

Synthetic bags are improving every year, and they are champs in wet conditions. Even if they get wet, they'll still keep you warm (not exactly comfortable, mind you, but far warmer than a wet down bag). Synthetics are also a good choice for kids and newcomers to camping, because they are less expensive than down and require minimum care.

The threads in synthetics are composed of extruded polymers, which is a fancy way of saying plastic. The threads are most commonly a continuous filament (a long, single strand), but they can also be arranged in short "staples" up to 4 inches long. Usually the threads are hollow, reducing their weight and enabling the bags to trap more air. Sheets of the insulation are layered on top of one another in different directions to prevent cold spots.

SLEEPING BAG INSULATION COMPARED

PROS	CONS
DOWN	
Lightweight, high warmth-to-volume ratio Highly compressible Maintains loft, lasts 3–4 times as long as synthetic Conforms to body for closer fit, better heat retention	Does not insulate when damp/wet Dries slowly Less insulation on underside because of compressibility Non-hypoallergenic Expensive
SYNTHETIC	
Stays warm when wet Dries quickly Hypoallergenic Less expensive than down	Heavier, lower warmth-to-volume ratio Bulkier, not as compressible as down Loft/insulating power degrades faster than down, especially with frequent washings Doesn't breathe as well as natural fibers; can feel clammy Doesn't conform to body like down

The most popular synthetic material is Polarguard. It is available in various grades, including:

▶ **Polarguard 3D:** *This product features a finer filament, a softer feel, and greater compressibility than previous generations of Polarguard.*

▶ **Polarguard HV:** *Not as light or compressible as 3D, HV is now found in budget level bags.*

Hybrid Bags

If you want the best of both worlds, check out synthetic-down combo bags. By utilizing a moisture-resistant synthetic fill on the underside of the bag, and down on the top, you get a bag that stays warm despite any ground moisture, yet has many of the benefits of down.

Shell and Liner

Shell and liner fabrics hold the filling in place—the shell on the outside, the liner on the inside. The shell should be tear resistant, cleanable, and water repellent but capable of allowing moisture inside the bag to evaporate. For the liner, you want something that feels good against your skin.

Most sleeping bag external shells are made of the following materials:

▶ **Ripstop:** *A lightweight polyester or nylon that incorporates a reinforced fiber mesh to prevent tearing.*

▶ **Taffeta:** *A smooth, light, almost silky type of nylon. Nicer than ripstop next to your skin.*

▶ **Dryloft:** *From the makers of Gore-Tex, this highly breathable, water resistant material protects the bag's shell and filling from ice, snow, dampness, and condensation. It can handle light rain but not heavy downpours.*

▶ **Polyester:** *This fabric is used in lower-cost bags. It tends to be heavy and bulky.*

▶ **Polyester Taffeta:** *this lightweight fabric is durable and easy to clean.*

Liners are made with some of the same materials as shells, such as ripstop nylon and polyester taffeta, with added emphasis on softness to enhance comfort. Cotton flannel and silk liners are popular choices because of their pleasurable feel next to the skin.

Internal Structure

The distribution of insulation in a bag depends on how it is held in place. In better-quality down bags, the insulation is evenly distributed through the use of baffles. In above-average synthetic bags, either shingle construction or offset quilted layers are used.

The goal in bag construction is to avoid cold spots. Quality down bags do this by using slant-walled baffles to keep the down in place; the walls of the baffles are angled so each section partially overlaps the adjacent baffle. Sometimes the user wants to move the down around to suit the conditions. With a continuous baffle that wraps around the entire bag, you can shake the bag to shift more down to the top layer (for cold nights) or the bottom (for warm evenings). For cold weather, you don't want the down to shift. Internal side block baffles, common on the sides of winter bags, block down from migrating out of position.

In lesser-quality bags, manufacturers use sew-through stitching, where the insulation is sandwiched between the shell and the lining, then stitched in place with thread that passes through all three layers. This creates long stitch marks where the bag is very thin. These are potential cold spots that can make for teeth chattering in the backcountry.

Additional Features

The features listed on store packaging can be confusing. Here are some terms you may encounter while shopping for sleeping bags:

▶ **Draft Tubes:** *As mentioned earlier, a bag should have at least one, and better two, draft tubes that run alongside the zipper to prevent warm air from escaping.*

down-filled/polyester-filled sewn-through

box-wall

slant-wall

overlapping tubes

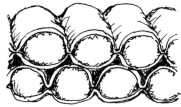

double-construction

shingle

Sleeping bag insulation. (Elara Tanguy)

▶ **Box foot:** *An expanded area at end of the bag for your feet. One notable example is the Shark's Toe, introduced by Mountain Equipment. The upper part of the bag is 5 centimeters longer than the lower, so your feet can relax in their most natural position when you're lying on your back.*

▶ **Differential cut:** *The inner lining is cut smaller than the outer shell, allowing insulation to loft up to its maximum. Ensures that the insulation layers will hold warmth and not compress.*

▶ **Differential fill:** *More insulation fills the top-side of the bag than the underside.*

▶ **Collar:** *A big neck gasket (located at shoulder level inside the sleeping bag) that helps hold heat inside the bag. Sometimes featuring a draw cord. Usually found in cold-weather sleeping bags and some three-season synthetic bags.*

▶ **Pad loops:** *Sewn-in straps that attach to your sleeping pad. This keeps you*

from rolling off the pad in the middle of the night.

▶ **Pillow pocket**: *A compartment built in to the head end of the bag that can be stuffed with clothing so you have a soft, cushy spot to rest your head.*

▶ **Utility pocket:** *A compartment for items such as car keys, a flashlight, mp3 player, or similar items.*

SHOPPING FOR A SLEEPING BAG

As you embark on your hunt for a sleeping bag, remember that the devil is in the details. Pay attention to design features and materials. Look at the foot section, hood area, and and zipper baffle (draft tube). How are they designed? Are there any obvious cold spots? How do these features compare with those on other bags? How much insulation is in the bag?

If you are buying your bag at a specialty store, the salespeople expect you to climb in and check it out. At a big-box store, on the other hand, tucking yourself in can look a little strange. Purchasing via the Internet is recommended only for experienced outdoor enthusiasts.

Study the Stitching

The stitching should be impeccable, with at least eight stitches to the inch and reinforcements at all stress points. Can you easily push the down out of the bag? (The foot of the bag, between the stitching, is a good place to test.) If down is coming out, the bag will lose its loft over time.

Get in the Bag

Make sure that there's enough room to be comfortable. Can you at least scratch your tummy? Pull on the drawscords and cinch the hood. Evaluate every aspect of the bag for comfort. Don't just try the bag lying on your back coffin style. If you sleep on your side or stomach, try the bag in those positions.

Play with the Zipper

On bags where the zipper opens completely, is it easy to mate the zipper again? Look for a bag that has an anti-snagging feature to prevent the zipper from catching the draft tubes.

If you are a backpacker or a cyclist, you might consider a three-quarter zipper to save an ounce or two. A three-quarter zipper is also a nice feature in a winter bag, because it's less drafty. For a three-season bag, however, it's better to buy a bag with a zipper that extends all the way down one side, to provide your feet some ventilation on warm nights.

Test the Loft

Stuff the bag into its stuff sack. Once compressed, will the bag fit comfortably within your backpack? Let the bag sit in its stuff sack for about five minutes, then take it out. Give it a good shake, lay out the bag on the ground, and give it about five minutes

to loft out. When it returns to its advertised loft, push down on each section, then let go. The bag should recover back to full height in a few seconds.

ACCESSORIES

Removable Liners

Pause for a moment and think about how dirty a sleeping bag gets trip after trip, year after year. It's enough to give you the creeps. At the same time, if you're like me, you might not relish washing your sleeping bag too often. The solution is a removable liner. An insert is basically an additional liner that fits inside the bag to protect the bag's original liner from sweat and body oils. The additional liner also provides a bit more warmth (up to 15 degrees Fahrenheit).

Removable liners come in a variety of materials, including nonwoven nylon, cotton and Egyptian cotton, silk, and flannel.

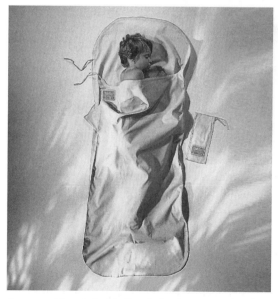

A removable, washable liner helps keep your sleeping bag clean. (Cocoon by Design Salt)

Stuff Sack

A sturdy and waterproof stuff sack protects your sleeping bag from the elements. When backpacking in wet climates, use a plastic bag as well, to be doubly sure. Look for a stuff sack with compression straps to reduce bulk.

Pillow

A pillow that packs small and expands big will enhance your campsite comfort. The Therm-A-Rest compressible pillow works well for both trekkers and car campers. Another good choice is the Slumberjack Quallo camp pillow, with a poly-cotton flannel cover and warm synthetic fill. My favorite is Cocoon's contour travel pillow, which compresses for tight packing, then bounces back to a comfy headrest.

SLEEPING BAG MAINTENANCE

Love your sleeping bag as I do mine. Don't snooze under the stars without first protecting your bag with a ground cloth. Otherwise, dirt and grit will begin to fray your bag's shell. Hang your bag after a trip so air can circulate through it. Above all, don't store your bag in a tight compression sack. If tightly compressed over long periods, your bag will lose its loft.

PADS, MATTRESSES, AND COTS

You will need something between your sleeping bag and the bottom of your tent for two reasons: insulation and padding. When you lie down in your bag, the insulation beneath you compresses. Down compresses virtually flat; synthetics compress less. That compression equals a loss of insulating power, and it also makes your body acutely aware of any rocks, twigs, and roots beneath you.

Sleeping Pads

A comfortable sleeping pad can mean the difference between a successful trip and a bummer. This protective layer cushions you, and also keeps you warm by insulating you from the cold ground.

If you are a back sleeper, you can probably get away with much less padding than if you are a side sleeper. Curvy women, especially side sleepers, tend to need more padding.

Three-quarter-length pads are ideal for smaller people or anyone who curls up when sleeping. Ounce-counting backpackers should also consider either these or mummy-shaped pads, which use less material and therefore save weight. When using a short pad in mild weather, you can insulate your feet from the ground with a strategically placed empty backpack or extra clothing.

In severe cold or snow camping, a full-length pad is a must, although a short pad can also serve a role. Many winter campers bring along two pads for extra insulation.

There are three options in sleeping pads: closed-cell foam, open-cell foam, and self-inflating pads. All come in different lengths and thickness, from short, thin foam pads that weigh only a few ounces to full-length self-inflators that weigh more than five pounds.

Though more spartan than self-inflating pads, foam pads have the advantage of being lightweight and inexpensive. Full-length pads weigh less than a pound, and short pads may be a half pound or less. Plus, you can leave a foam pad on the ground without worrying about damage.

Closed-Cell Foam Pads

Closed-cell pads are made out of dense foam filled with tiny closed air cells. They are impervious to water and are a good choice for lightweight, durable, and inexpensive insulation.

Closed-cell pads are bulkier than self-inflators, and they do not offer much cushioning. Some

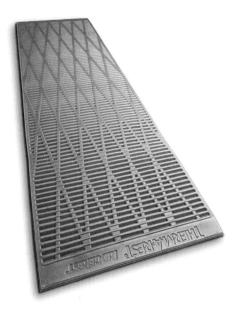

Closed-cell foam pad. (Therm-a-Rest)

The Power Lounger is a sleeping pad that easily converts to a camp chair. (Crazy Creek)

manufacturers have improved on the comfort aspect by adding ridges, which allow more softness and give. One of the most comfortable of these is the Ridge-Rest from Cascade Designs. Another innovative design is the Power Lounger, from Crazy Creek. This fabric-covered, closed-cell foam pad folds rather than rolls up. Buckling a strap on each side quickly converts it into a camping chair or a canoe seat.

Open-Cell Foam Pads

Open-cell foam pads are made of the same kind of foam used in couch cushions, so they're more comfortable than closed-cell foam pads. They range from 1 to 2 inches thick, with thicker pads being more comfortable.

Like their closed-cell counterparts, open-cell pads are bulky. They also absorb water. Even though most are covered with waterproof material on the bottom and breathable material on the top, moisture still gets trapped in the pad during rainy weather. Many campers—particularly campers with synthetic sleeping bags—are willing to put up with this problem in order to get two full inches of softness that an open-cell pad can offer.

A self-inflating pad insulates you from the ground and provides restful cushioning. (Therm-a-Rest)

PADS, COTS, AND MATTRESSES COMPARED

WEIGHT	PRICE	PROS	CONS
OPEN-CELL PAD			
1½ lbs.–8 lbs.	$25–$100	Cushiony, comfortable Lightweight Highly effective insulator Inexpensive	Bulky; difficult to compress Less insulating than closed-cell Absorbs water Not very durable
CLOSED-CELL PAD			
7½ oz.–4½ lbs.	$15–$20	Lightweight Effective insulator Puncture proof Doesn't absorb water Inexpensive	Bulky, difficult to compress Stiff and firm
SELF-INFLATING PAD			
1½ lbs.–8 lbs.	$50–$160	Adjustable firmness Effective insulator except on snow Extremely compact when rolled	Subject to punctures Expensive
AIR MATTRESS			
8 lbs.–35 lbs.	$30–$100	Very comfortable Inexpensive	Heavy and bulky Poor insulator Subject to punctures Requires air pump Time consuming to set up
COT			

6 lbs.–23 lbs.	$39–$90	Very comfortable
		Raises sleeper above wet ground
		  and any critters
		Space saver, can stow gear
		  underneath
			Heavy, bulky, awkward to carry
			Poor insulator; allows air circulation
			  underneath
			Legs can damage tent fabric
			Cot material can sag after
			  extended use

An open-cell foam pad is lightweight and inexpensive. It compresses better than one made of closed-cell foam. (Therm-a-Rest)

Self-Inflating Pads

When it comes to comfort, self-inflating pads offer quality snoozing. Unroll one of these pads, then watch it inflate by itself. Add a few puffs of breath to adjust the firmness to your liking.

Self-inflaters come in a variety of thicknesses and lengths. Some have no-slip surfaces to keep you from sliding off. Some incorporate down for improved insulation and comfort. (Exped's Down

Air Mattress, for example, includes a plush layer of 700 fill power down.)

Although self-inflaters are two to three times pricier than foam pads, they're immensely popular among backcountry travelers for some very good reasons: they are just plain cushy and they roll up tight. Self-inflating mattresses take a bit more care than other pads. They can be punctured, and the valves may eventually wear out and leak. For these reasons, it's necessary to carry a repair kit.

Consider camping with a closed-cell pad for thermal efficiency as well as a self-inflating mattress, keeping the closed-cell foam pad on top. That's the pad that will better prevent the loss of heat.

Air Mattresses

Talk about comfort! Air mattresses (also called air beds) look like the familiar mattress/box spring combination, but air provides the support. There are many varieties of camping air mattresses. A few have a velour top or a padded removable surface for added comfort, and a built-in air pump for convenience. Some air mattresses are battery powered, but a better solution is a rechargeable pump.

An air mattress is not an effective insulator. One solution is to put a wool blanket on top of the air mattress and your sleeping bag on top of that. (Wool is an excellent insulator.)

Cots

For comfort, there's no substitute for a good-quality camping cot. Sleeping on a cot keeps you away from ground moisture and unwelcome critters.

On the downside, cots are bulkier and heavier than sleeping pads, so they're not for the weight-conscious backpacker. And they don't insulate well because air circulates underneath them.

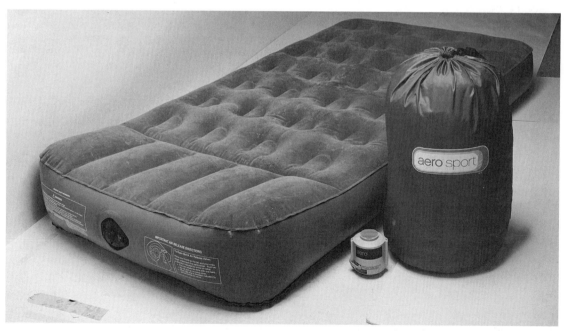

An air mattress is a popular choice for car campers who want lots of cushioning underneath and aren't concerned about weight or space. (L.L. Bean)

Camping cots provide a raised surface that offers more comfort and more warmth than sleeping on the ground. Some models come with organizers that hang off the side of the cot to keep personal items within reach. (The Coleman Company, Inc.)

CHAPTER 5

BACKPACKS

Backpacks come in all shapes and sizes. Whether you're in the market for a daypack, a weekender, or a thru-hiker's pack, you should choose your gear carefully. Some backpackers relish a no-frills ultralight pack. Others, like me, prefer a little more padding; even if it adds extra weight. Thanks to recent advances, the days of heavy shoulder-gouging backpacks are long gone. Packs now come with a variety of straps and support systems that make the load less burdensome.

BACKPACKS 101

In the old days, packs made of cotton canvas, waterproofed with a wax coating, were popular because of their excellent water resistance, but the fabric was heavy and prone to abrasion and would rot if not perfectly dry when stored. Today the preferred fabric is strong, abrasion-resistant nylon.

Runners-up are Cordura and Kolan—lightweight yet rough, fuzzy, and abrasion-resistant fabrics. Neither is as puncture resistant as some other nylons, but they are considered waterproof.

Most of today's backpacks, regardless of their materials, have a waterproof coating on the inside as well as on the seams. If you're caught in a downpour, however, the outside fabric will likely get soaked and water will seep in around the zippers. Any moisture that gets inside stays inside. So always use a pack cover (or a plastic garbage bag) in foul weather to block rainwater completely. (Gregory Mountain Products makes excellent rain covers in five different models to fit the wide range of backpacks on the market.)

Daypacks

Daypacks are ubiquitous because of their utility value; they can carry books, groceries, and gear in the woods. For trail use, a daypack is for what the name implies; it is large enough to hold what you'll likely need for a day trip. The pack should be easy to

GOING SOLAR

Consumer electronics are becoming more energy efficient with each passing year—so much so that many battery-powered items can be recharged by solar power.

Enter the solar backpack.

Solar backpacks are the wave of the future. With their generators soaking up the sun, they allow you to use your small electrical gear while being liberated from a socket. Lightweight, waterproof solar panels are stitched onto the outside of the pack and can generate up to 4 watts of power. This allows you to recharge items such as a small lantern, a flashlight, or an mp3 player while you hike.

You can also buy a separate solar panel that can be placed on a picnic table, tent, or anywhere else in your campsite.

Daypacks are a smart choice for day walks. They aren't much use for backpacking unless you are an ultra-lightweight gear freak. A padded hip belt and padded, contoured shoulder straps contribute to their comfort. Easy-access pockets are good for storing a camera, GPS receiver, or other items you want to keep protected yet accessible. (Johnson Outdoors, Inc.)

load and have some external pockets, some lash points for extra items, padded shoulder straps, and a waist strap for stability. Daypacks don't have a frame, as do most larger backpacks. Rucksacks (larger-capacity day packs) are a good option for short overnight trips.

Thru-Hiker Backpacks

External-Frame Packs

Woefully out of favor for many years, external-frame packs are staging a comeback. A well-built, well-fitted external-frame pack is a smart choice if you are a backpacker who stays mostly on well-maintained trails over moderate terrain.

An external frame pack is an oldie design but it's going to stick around. The ridged frame is usually made of tubular aluminum alloy consisting of two curved vertical bars that hold the pack away from the back. The design shows its merits during summer months and strenuous hikes because it provides a space away from the back, permitting sweat to dissipate. A system of straps and pads keeps the pack away from the back, which minimizes chafing and allows ventilation.

External-frame packs are easy to pack. Multiple tie-on points facilitate gear attachment, and separate compartments make for convenient organization. Multiple compartments also make it easy to evenly distribute the load.

Solar backpack. (Voltaic Systems)

Solar panel. (Everlite)

An external-frame backpack. (The Coleman Company, Inc.)

Some of these benefits can be drawbacks, however. Because the pack sits away from your back, it can throw you off balance on uneven terrain. Gear lashed on the outside of the pack is exposed to weather and sharp objects. And although you can distribute weight in the pack, the external-frame design means that overall the pack has a higher center of gravity and can be top-heavy.

Internal-Frame Packs

An internal frame pack has none of the instability that encumbers hikers on rugged terrain. Though hotter than an external-frame pack (because it rests directly on your back) and more difficult to pack and organize, it is more maneuverable in tight spaces and offers better balance because the pack doesn't bounce around.

There are trade-offs with internal-frame packs, however. They're often top-loading and come with fewer compartments than external-frame packs,

TREKKING POLES

Telescoping aluminum walking poles help you distribute the weight of your pack throughout your body. They extend the hiking day considerably by easing the strain on your knees and feet.

Trekking poles help the hiker maintain her rhythm while she negotiates tough terrain. Backpackers like them because they relieve the weight on the feet and back, thus saving some energy while on long hikes. Retractable, they can be stashed in your pack. (Adrienne Hall)

An internal-frame backpack. (The Coleman Company, Inc.)

ANATOMY OF A BACKPACK

Hip Belt

Although your shoulders and back do a decent share of the work, the hip belt transfers the bulk of the load to your hips. A good hip belt should have at least 1/4 inch of foam padding. (Some hip belts are made of seat-belt webbing, which doesn't provide much comfort.) Belts come in several sizes for a custom fit.

making them more difficult to organize and repack when moving camp. Also, an internal-frame pack sits directly on your back, sharply reducing ventilation—a serious drawback in hot climates.

BACKPACK COMFORT COMPARISON

PACK	WEIGHT	PRICE	PROS	CONS	BEST USE
Top loading	2 lbs. 4 oz.–6.2 lbs.	$69–$450	More capacity	Less convenient access	For carrying more gear than a panel loading pack
Panel loading (unzips on sides)	2 lbs. 4 oz.–6 lbs.	$119–$350	Easy access. Allows you to better organize your gear inside. Lets you see all the contents of your pack at once	Gear can spring out if packed tightly. Cannot overstuff for risk of bursting a zipper. Zippers can jam or break if the pack is too full. Can't cram as much stuff in as you would a top-loader	For trips when you need to frequently access your gear
External frame	3 lbs. 6 oz.–6 lbs.	$70–$469	More comfortable for long trips, hot weather. Easy to pack; better weight distribution. Can carry heavier loads. Accommodates bulky items well (tent, sleeping bag). Frames often adjustable, allowing you to shift weight up or down for added comfort so more weight can be carried more comfortably	Can be top-heavy. Cumbersome when walking in tight spaces	Hiking well-traveled, well-maintained trails. Longer trips. Because less expensive, good choice for children and beginning campers
Internal frame	2 lbs. 2 oz.–6 lbs. –6 oz.	$108–$359	Excellent stability. Allows more range of motion. More compact load. Designed to custom fit the wearer. Works well for nearly everyone	Limited air circulation between back and pack. Requires care in packing for even weight distribution	Uneven terrain. Off-trail hiking

Shoulder Straps

The shoulders carry as much as a quarter of the pack's weight. Well-padded shoulder straps make carrying your load more comfortable. Wider shoulder straps are less likely to pinch your skin.

Sternum Strap

The sternum strap, or chest strap, connects the two shoulder straps. It should buckle across your sternum just below your collarbones. The sternum strap helps bring the weight of the load forward and reduces pack wobble.

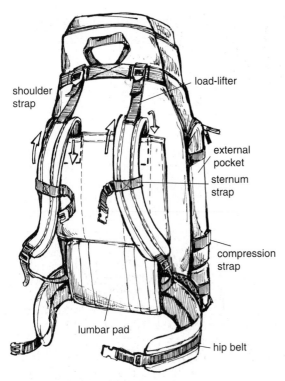

Backpack features. (Elara Tanguy)

shoulder strap
load-lifter
external pocket
sternum strap
compression strap
lumbar pad
hip belt

HYDRATION SYSTEM

Many backpacks come with a built-in water bladder or have a special pocket to accommodate a water bladder and drinking tube.

Hydration pack. (Camelbak)

Load Lifters

Load lifters attach from the shoulder straps to the top of the frame (both internal and external). They adjust the weight balance for shoulder and hip relief, and they control pack sway and the distance between the pack and the suspension. The optimal angle is 45 degrees.

Compression Straps

Compression straps constrict the bulk of the pack to hold the contents in place and prevent sudden weight shifts. They can also be used to lash sleeping pads and wet rain gear to the outside of the pack. When packing, start with the compression straps loosened, then tighten them after you've loaded the pack.

Lumbar Pad or Contoured Back

Most packs come with either a lumbar pad or a contoured back. A foam lumbar pad protects the small of your back from the frame and the lumpy contents of the pack. A contoured back serves the same purpose. Either one improves your posture, which helps your body shoulder the burden, so to speak.

BUYING THE RIGHT PACK

One of the most important considerations when buying a pack is getting the right size for your needs and for your body. Don't buy a large pack just because you think it's impressive when a medium-size one will do. You want a backpack that is just big enough to contain all your gear. If a backpack is too large or too small, the weight might not be distributed evenly and, believe me, you will be uncomfortable. Says Gina DeMillo, associate editor for *Backpacker* magazine, "If it's too short, it probably won't be resting on your hips. It will be tugging at your shoulders and you'll feel a lot of weight there. If it's too big, the belt will hit you below the hip. In other words, it should be proportional to your body size."

Most important, make sure the pack you choose is comfortable before you buy it. Don't wait until you're on the trail to discover that the pack shifts around on your back or puts the weight on your shoulders instead of your hips. Try out as many different backpack styles as you can before you make your decision. Comfort rules, so don't be unnecessarily swayed by snazzy colors or features. Take all the time you need to find a backpack that's right for you.

Capacity

Here's one way to estimate the capacity you need: Assemble everything you will take on the trip. Place these items in a large plastic garbage bag and

measure, in inches, the height, width, and length of the filled bag. Multiply these numbers to determine the cubic inches of volume you require for your pack. American manufacturers list pack size by cubic inches; other companies measure volume in cubic liters, so make the conversion before you go pack shopping.

Fit

After you know how much capacity you'll need, narrow the options to a pack that fits. The fit of the frame is crucial to comfort: we know a poor-fitting pair of shoes can ruin a hiking trip, but the wrong backpack can sink a trip to a new level of hell.

The right pack size depends on your torso length, or *drop*, and your overall height. The drop is measured from the bony protrusion at the base of the neck to your waist (at the top of your hip bones).

Many packs help you achieve a good fit through a vertically adjustable suspension system tailored to your torso.

Methods vary for torso adjustment, from ladder-lock systems to adjustable hip belts to elongating shoulder straps. Recently, manufacturers have begun making packs specifically for women. Women typically have a shorter torso and narrower shoulders than men.

THERE'S COMFORT IN NUMBERS

Backpacking in a group has many benefits. Not only does a group share a wonderful experience, but they also share the burden of carrying gear and completing chores.

Communication is key when assembling a group. Everyone should be in agreement on hiking speed, distance per day, and food choices.

Not having any backpacking friends need not be an impediment, because many organizations can help ease your way into the sport. Not-for-profit membership organizations such as the Appalachian Mountain Club have local

chapters all over the country that organize multiple trips every year. Some trips are rigorous; others are perfect for beginners. You'll be with like-minded campers who are usually eager to share information and welcome you into the sport.

Hundreds of private outfitters and guide services offer a variety of self-directed and guided trips ranging from beginner to expert level. Because these companies live and die on good customer service and word-of-mouth recommendations, they'll do their best to help you select an appropriate trek for your skill level.

Signs of Quality

Even if a pack fits you like a glove, it won't do you much good if it falls apart in the middle of nowhere. When shopping around, look closely at the stitches on the pack, and apply some pressure to the seams. Gaps between stitches or broken threads are tip-offs that the pack is substandard. Make sure the seams are properly stitched and there are no signs of frayed material.

Keep your eyes open for smart features. Quick-release clasps secure your gear yet provide easy access. Adjustable flaps allow you to expand or compress the load. A rain cover keeps your pack dry. Lash points and punched-leather patches on the outside of the pack let you attach extra gear. These are all standard features on a good pack.

Test Drive

Specialty retailers often provide you with weights to test the pack in the store. Put about 25 pounds of weight into the pack, then walk around to see how it feels. No part of the pack should be uncomfortable. The hip belt should fit firmly around your hips and carry most of the weight. Test the fit by lifting a knee; if the movement disturbs the pack, chances are that the hip belt is either too high or too low.

The shoulder straps should not cut into your armpits. The pack should not bounce against your back when you walk.

A sales clerk should be able to fine-tune the pack's fit. This isn't something you can do alone, so welcome the extra pair of hands.

A properly fitted and adjusted pack should put nearly all the weight on your hips; your shoulder straps will merely keep the pack from falling backward.

As you walk around the store, jog at times and jump up and down. Stretch over forward and touch your toes. Raise and lower a leg onto a bench or chair, then jostle your body from side to side. The pack should move with you and not throw you off balance. If it moves around on your back, try readjusting it. If that doesn't work, move on to another pack.

PACKING

In his book *A Fine and Pleasant Misery,* Patrick McManus writes, "The rule of thumb for the old backpacking was that the weight of your pack should equal the weight of yourself and the kitchen sink combined. Just a casual glance at the full pack sitting on the floor could give you a double hernia and fuse four vertebrae."

Thankfully, the mantra for backpacking has changed to "lighten up." Weight-watching backpackers can stay warm, dry, and well-fed for a full week in the wilderness with less than 20 pounds on their back.

If you're less disciplined—and most of us are—you'll probably carry a bit more than 20 pounds.

So what's the upper limit? A good rule of thumb is to carry no more than one-third of your body weight.

QUICK TIP: PACK SOME PACKS

Bring a day pack for each person old enough to wear one, even if you don't plan on trekking any distance. Children can use their school day packs for short walks and hikes and as containers for their possessions such as toys, coloring books, crayons, and travel games. A waist pouch or fanny pack are also useful to carry snacks and a few essentials for short walks.

BACKPACKING GEAR AND GIZMOS

ITEM	PRICE
Backpacking chair (sleeve for self-inflating pad)	$39–$49
Trekking poles	$89–$109/pair
Solar shower	$19–$29
Global positioning system (GPS) unit	$99–$559
Cook kit	$19–$80
Hand shovel	$15–$30
Digital compass	$30–$45
Headlamp	$20–$55
Pack towel	$6–$24
Personal water purifier	$90–$130
Java press	$14–$20
Multi-tool/knife	$14–$35
Solar panel	$30–$129

You'll save yourself a lot of time and potential discomfort by referring to a comprehensive packing list (see Appendix A: Camping Checklists). Consider it a starting point for preparing for your trip.

Organizing Your Pack

When it comes to packing, everybody's got an opinion. Though pack designs vary considerably, the keys to achieving comfort remain the same: pack heavier items toward the bottom, lighter items at the top, and evenly distribute the weight from side to side.

When it's time to pack, collect everything and lay it out on the floor. If you're going with a friend or a group, sort out shared equipment (e.g., tent and cooking gear) into a pile then divide the items among each person. Now divide all your items into two piles: 1) items that you'll only need while at camp; 2) items you'll need on the trail or for emergencies. Pack everything from Pile 1 first, then pack Pile 2 on top or in the side pockets.

Once you've packed everything, take a long walk with the pack on your back. If it's too heavy, remove any non-essential items and try again.

GET IN SHAPE . . . AND GO!

One general bit of advice before you go: get in shape. Can you comfortably hike 6 to 8 miles in one day with a full pack? How would you hold up in a group that wants to go 12 miles or more in one day? Can you walk 4 miles straight without a break, without carrying a pack? What about 8 miles in four hours? If you've been sitting at the computer too long (as I was when I wrote this book), start aiming for these goals a few months before your trip. The fitter you are, the more comfortable you'll be on the trail and in camp at day's end.

CHAPTER 6

CLOTHING AND FOOTWEAR

Back in the early 1950s when Sir Edmund Hillary was planning his conquest of Mount Everest, he wanted clothes that would provide warmth in extreme conditions. He wore down clothing with windproof outerwear, high-assault boots (that got wet and froze solid), and three pairs of gloves (silk, woolen, and windproof). He also contrived a homemade sun hat.

Today, Hillary could easily find more suitable gear from any local outfitter. Technology, fit, and fabrics have all changed dramatically since his time and much to the better for the most part. Not

only do today's performance fabrics wick and breathe, they are wind- and waterproof, tear resistant, quick drying, easy to care for, and able to block sun and bugs.

Still, if Hillary tried to buy a parka today, he might be as flummoxed as the rest of us, because the new technology comes with its own arcane vocabulary. Words like polypropylene, hydrophobic, and Primaloft don't roll easily off the tongue. Today Hillary, who endorses both polypropylene and wool, contends ". . . clothing is a lot more efficient than it ever was in my day."

FABRIC LINGO

Breathability describes the extent to which air moves through a fabric. This helps determine its capacity to resist wind, retain body heat, and aid in moisture management. A breathable fabric allows sweat vapors to escape. But there is a trade-off between breathability and water resistance: usually the more of one, the less of the other.

Coating pertains to synthetic rubber or polyurethane that is applied to a fabric for waterproofing or wind resistance.

FABRIC LINGO (*continued*)

Continuous filament describes fabrics made up of continuous fibers. They are used primarily in synthetic insulation, such as Polarguard.

Dead air space is found within filaments such as goose down. Most often found in outerwear, dead-air space prevents air from moving, thus retaining heat.

Heavyweight fabric, also known as *expedition weight*, is often used in base layers, such as long underwear. Heavyweight fabric usually has a brushed finish on the inside for warmth and wicking, and a smooth outer surface that resists pilling.

Hydrophilic, or *water loving*, describes the wicking characteristics of fibers. As the name suggests, hydrophilic fibers are highly absorbent.

Hydrophobic, or *water hating*, describes moisture-repellent fibers. Such fibers are often paired with hydrophilic fibers to create a push-pull action to move moisture away from your body and toward the surface of the fabric for rapid evaporation.

Lamination seals one fabric to another with heat, adhesives, and pressure. Laminated fabrics are more durable than coated fabrics.

Lightweight fabrics are best suited for highly aerobic, cool-weather pursuits. they are often used in base layers, such as long underwear.

Microfibers are extremely fine, tightly woven fibers that combine natural breathability with wind and water resistance. Used in performance outerwear, microfibers are often laminated to a waterproof/breathable fabric or treated with a waterproof/breathable coating.

Ripstop—usually made from nylon or polyester—blocks wind and water, and resists tearing. These qualities are better for tents than clothing; in damp weather they can feel clammy against your skin.

Seam sealing indicates that leak-proof tape or glue has been applied to the stitching (seams) of clothing or outdoor gear.

Vapor barrier is a layer of fabric added to outerwear that blocks water vapor from entering the clothing.

Ventilation describes openings in the clothing that permit heat and moisture to escape quickly.

Water-resistant clothing can repel water for short durations of mildly wet weather, but may eventually get soaked. Most nylon and other shell fabrics are water resistant, not waterproof.

Waterproof fabrics completely block the passage of water. Waterproof fabrics do not allow moisture to penetrate inward, but they can also prevent unwanted body moisture from escaping. For this reason, you should look for outerwear that is both waterproof *and* breathable.

Wicking describes a fabric's ability to pull moisture and sweat away from the skin and dispersing it throughout the material. This is a critical attribute in high-performance base layers.

Wind-resistant fabrics reduce the amount of wind that can penetrate your clothing. Wind-resistant clothing generally comes in the form of a lightweight outer layer that is both breathable and water-resistant.

Windproof fabrics block wind from penetrating your clothing, which sharply reduces the effects of windchill.

Take heart. You don't need a doctorate in chemistry, engineering, or physics to understand what's available, but you *do* need to develop a basic comprehension of how these fabrics work. Do your research, and get your money's worth (high-tech gear isn't cheap).

---■---

CLOTHING BASICS

Before you can select appropriate clothing for a camping trip, you have to know what kind of weather to expect—not just the expected high and low temperatures but the temperature changes that occur throughout the day. You should also anticipate the amount and type of precipitation you might encounter during the trip. State tourism bureaus and weather websites can provide a lot of useful information.

Also consider how much of that weather you'll actually be exposed to. If an all-day rain is predicted, will you still be in transit to your destination or asleep in your tent rather than out hiking on the trail? If sunny, windy conditions are forecast, will you be hiking in dense forest rather than open ridges, exposed to the sun and wind? How long is your trip? How many changes of clothing can you carry, and are there laundry facilities along the way? (And how long can you stand *not* laundering your clothes?)

Natural and Synthetic Fibers

Although natural fibers sound appealing, they have some dangerous deficiencies compared to synthetics. Their lack of performance can compromise your comfort and safety, especially when the weather turns ugly. In general, synthetics provide better performance, and campers who value comfort favor them in most situations. Below is a rundown of the most popular choices in both categories, with natural fibers first.

Cotton

A highly absorbent natural fabric that is comfortable next to the skin, cotton provides a quick cooling effect that is refreshing on a hot day. But in winter, cotton is basically useless. It wicks water away from the skin, but, unlike polypropylene, cotton retains the moisture, and eliminates the dead-air space within the fabric. So, unlike fibers that maintain dead-air space when soaked, cotton will not keep you warm when wet. If you're in a cold, unforgiving climate, wet cotton can make you susceptible to hypothermia (hence the old adage, "cotton kills").

Down

Down filling is not just for sleeping bags; it is one of the most popular choices for camping clothes. It is naturally warm, soft, and light when dry. It molds to your body, helping to keep you warm while absorbing any moisture. Its absorptive properties can be a liability, however, if you will be in very wet and cold conditions. Once the down in your jacket gets wet, the down collapses into clumps and loses its insulating qualities.

Rayon

Rayon is a combination of cellulose of wood pulp (usually pine, spruce, or hemlock) and cotton linters or cotton. Cotton linters are residue fibers which cling to cotton seed after the ginning process. It is a popular fabric in outdoor clothing due to its low cost.

Silk

Silk is lightweight, cool, and extremely comfortable, but it is expensive and requires delicate care. Its use in outdoor clothing is primarily limited to liners for gloves, and in socks and underwear. Silk is particularly effective as an insulator because of its hollow fibers; therefore it retains some insulation value even when wet.

Wool

Wool is a natural fabric made from the hair of various animals, but predominantly sheep. It is nature's techno-fabric. The insulation value of wool can be a godsend in an unexpected snowstorm. Although wool insulates even when wet, it is bulky, shrinks easily, can be scratchy, absorbs water quickly, and has an unpleasant odor when wet. Plus, when wool clothing takes in water it becomes very heavy. Wool camping clothes purchased at a surplus store are relatively inexpensive.

Capilene (Patagonia)
This is Patagonia's polyester base layer fabric. The fabric surface is treated to make it hydrophilic, whereas the core remains hydrophobic. This combination wicks water away from the skin without soaking the fiber.

Coolmax (Invista)
When your clothing gets wet and sticks to your skin, it stops the evaporation process that keeps the skin cool. Coolmax was developed to keep an air space between you and the garment next to your skin to facilitate evaporation. The fabric was originally designed to keep soldiers and police officers cool in their uniforms.

Cordura (DuPont)
This is one tough fabric that looks and feels like cotton canvas, but it outperforms and outlasts cotton canvas by years. Although it weighs half as much as cotton duck fabric, it has three times the tear strength and three times the abrasion resistance.

Fleece, or Pile
One of the most versatile fabrics offered today, fleece is often made of plastic (polyester, polypropylene, et cetera). Fleece is light weight, warm when wet, and can be used as a mid- or outer layer. Fleece also helps move moisture outward to keep you dry. Fleece is available in heavyweight, midweight, and lightweight options. A base layer, for example, would utilize lightweight, single-layer construction; it is sometimes brushed on the inside and smooth on the outside for increased warmth. The disadvantage of fleece is that it has very poor wind resistance.

Gore-Tex
Gore-Tex's eponymous product is the granddaddy of high-tech, breathable fabrics. It is generally used as a waterproof yet breathable membrane between other fabrics. It is found in rainwear, outerwear, skiwear, paddling garments, boots, and gloves. Nothing is perfect, however; although Gore-Tex is technically a breathable fabric, it can still feel a little stuffy.

Nylon
Nylon, a synthetic fiber, is used widely in outdoor clothing and gear. It is the major blending component of most high-tech fabrics, sometimes adding shine and always adding strength. It seems to bring out the best in cottons and polyesters while bonding well with coatings.

Polarguard
Polarguard's eponymous material is one of the original and most durable synthetic fillings used in sleeping bags and outerwear. Polarguard won't separate, mat, or clump, although items filled with it are somewhat bulky.

Polartec (Malden Mills)
This brand-name polyester fleece traps air warmed by exertion yet is breathable.

Polyester
This quick-drying, high-strength, and abrasion- and crease-resistant synthetic fiber is frequently blended with other synthetics or cotton or rayon.

Polypropylene
Polypropylene, or polypro, is hydrophobic, quick drying, colorfast, and retains heat. Polypro is the first synthetic to elbow aside cotton longjohns. Polypro has vastly improved since the days when it was known as a stinky fabric that was likely to pill, shrink, or shrivel when laundered. Polypropylene layers are extremely effective worn directly against the skin.

Polyurethane
Known for its flexibility, polyurethane is used in foams, elastomers (a macromolecular material having the elastic properties of natural rubber), and fabric coatings. Polyurethane coated fabrics are durable and abrasion-resistant, while also being

soft, light, and breathable. Polyurethane is also used to make Spandex (see below).

Primaloft/Primaloft 2 (Albany International)

Primaloft is a combination of large- and small-diameter polyester fibers intermingled to create a downlike feel. Soft and lofty, it is remarkably water resistant.

Spandex

A generic name for a synthetic fiber that offers great stretch and good strength, spandex also provides abrasion resistance and long-term resistance to body acids. It is always blended with another fiber, such as cotton, polyester, or nylon.

Supplex (DuPont)

A lightweight nylon fabric, Supplex has a dry, cottony feel. It's quick drying, tough yet soft, and versatile enough for uses ranging from running shorts to skiwear. With its high-wicking qualities, it is used to line other breathable fabrics.

Thinsulate (3M Corporation)

This polyester fiber insulation provides warmth without bulk. It is most often used in outerwear, footwear, and gloves because of its insulating efficiency.

Ultrex (Burlington Industries)

Ultrex is a waterproof, windproof, durable, and extremely breathable fabric coating. It provides extreme protection from a wide range of weather conditions.

COLD-WEATHER CLOTHING

Layering

Whether you are in warm or cold weather, you should dress in layers. Layering means putting on a number of breathable and moisture-managing layers that can be taken off one by one instead of one or two heavier layers. Comfort—a reasonable balance between heat loss and gain—is achieved by removing or adding layers as required. Well-chosen and versatile outdoor clothing as part of a layering system adapts to protect you from thermal stress, rain, snow, and wind.

Layered clothing systems are versatile and efficient. A number of thin layers will be warmer than one or two thick layers, and they'll take less room in your pack or duffel. Although not all garments can adapt to varying conditions or temperatures, you make it work by putting together flexible and complementary garments that contribute to your layered plan. When assembling your wardrobe, keep in mind that each layer performs a specific

THE BIRTH OF LAYERING

There's nothing new about layering. The idea of dressing in layers was the brainchild of Leon Leonwood Bean, the quintessential backwoods outdoorsman who parlayed his Maine outfitter store into a multimillion-dollar mail-order company. When escaping to Dew Drop Inn, his Maine hunting camp, he would start the day piling on clothes in a process he coined as "onionization." By strategically putting on and peeling off his clothes as the temperature rose, fell, and rose again during the course of the day, he maintained that he was not only keeping his body comfortable, but also providing a string of trail markers: As the sun climbed higher in the sky and he began to sweat, he'd doff a piece of clothing and drape it on a tree limb. By 3pm or so, when the woods grew chilly and he was only wearing two layers, he'd follow the trail of shirts and sweaters toward home. Along the way, he'd put on each article of clothing and arrive back at Dew Drop Inn safe and snug.

Base layer

Midlayer

long underwear top
(zipper neck)

lightweight fleece
top (zipper front)

wicking
underwear,
not cotton

wicking long
underwear
bottoms

noncotton
wicking socks

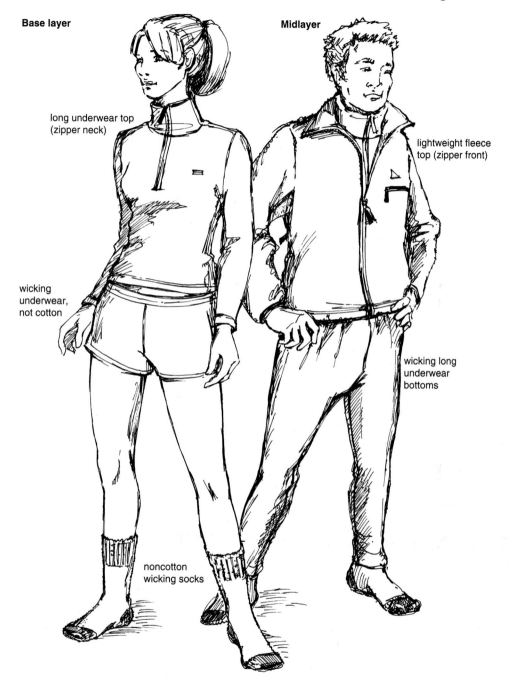

Layering is an essential key to comfort. Each layer has a function: the base manages moisture, the middle shields you from the cold, and the outer protects you from wind and rain. A layering system of clothing provides comfort and flexibility, allowing you to pack fewer pieces of apparel, which in turn enables you to maximize your weight and space allowance. (Elara Tanguy)

Outer layer

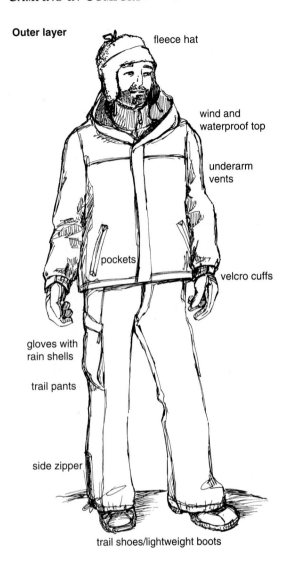

fleece hat

wind and
waterproof top

underarm
vents

pockets

velcro cuffs

gloves with
rain shells

trail pants

side zipper

trail shoes/lightweight boots

Rain wear

rain jacket with hood

rain pants

function (moisture management, warmth, protection from the elements) and none should hinder
mobility. Done right, you'll be set to go from the
beach to the mountains in the same day.

Base Layer

Your base layer should be a comfortable and thin
garment made of a wicking material that conforms
to your skin.

Mid-Layer

Depending on the water and air temperature, the
thickness of your mid-layer (or layers) will vary.

*Layering (continued). The outer layer is your defense
against wind and water. It should retain body heat
while letting water vapor out. Vents, storm flaps, draw-
cords, and fastenable cuffs are crucial to comfort.*

Naturally it should provide insulation and encourage moisture to move away from the body. Two or more garments in the insulating layer (shirts and sweaters) allow flexibility, because you can add or remove them as needed.

Outer Layer

Your outer layer is directly exposed to the elements, so it should be windproof. This layer protects and regulates the boundary of warm air around the body but also allows moisture vapors to escape. Waterproofing is another option you should consider. Your outer layer could be a simple shell, with no additional insulation, or it may have built-in insulation. This layer should have features such as draw cords and fastenable cuffs to prevent warm air escaping.

A wired jacket, such as the Victorinox Alchemist, not only serves as an outer layer, it's also equipped with battery-operated LED lights in its hood. The lights enhance peripheral and distance vision in the dark, allowing the user hands-free mobility. (Victorinox Swiss Army)

Headgear

Toes cold? Wear a hat. That's what the Inuits used to say. It's the simplest thing you can do to warm up in bracing weather. Bodies lose significant amounts of heat through the head and neck–and it can be dangerous.

A good hat not only heats up your noggin, it shields you from rain, sun, glare, flying beasties,

A wool cap (aka beanie) provides warmth and comfort without bulk. Use it as a night cap when you're tucked in your sleep bag. (Smart Wool)

A bomber hat will keep you sane and toasty in bracing weather. Insulated with either rabbit or fake fur, the ear flaps drop down for added warmth. (L.L. Bean)

Balaclavas. (PowderFish Mountain Apparel, LLC)

and other minor annoyances. If the weather is too mild for a heavy winter hat, consider an insulating headband instead.

In bitter cold, a convertible balaclava is the most versatile. Convertible balaclavas (see accompanying photo) can be worn as full head and neck protection, head protection only, or neck protection only. Synthetic face masks and helmet liners also provide exceptional warmth and keep the head dry.

A scarf or an insulated "neck gaiter" of some kind will insulate the neck and also keep warm air from "pumping" out of your outer layer during exertion. It will also stop wind-driven snow from sifting down into your clothing, where it can melt and cause discomfort.

Gloves and Mittens

The extremities can get very cold very quickly. Fingers and toes lose heat rapidly and are highly susceptible to frostbite, so pay particular attention to keeping them warm.

Mittens are warmer than gloves. Mittens allow your fingers to keep one another warm, unlike gloves which keep your fingers isolated. The trouble with mittens is that they limit your ability to manipulate objects. Gloves, on the other hand, allow for greater nimbleness.

The layering principle also applies to hands. Ideally you should have a light base layer, an insulating layer(s), and then a wind- and waterproof outer layer. If you are in snow country, mittens with long wrist cuffs, preferably reaching about halfway up the forearm, are recommended.

And if you're like me and get distracted by your outdoor activities, idiot strings (which attach your gloves to your jacket) will keep you from losing your gloves or mittens.

A low-bulk, wind-blocking neck gaiter delivers stretch and breathability to keep you dry, warm, and comfortable. A shaped neck gaiter enhances protection from the wind. (PowderFish Mountain Apparel, LLC)

Glove liners provide an extra layer of warmth next to your skin. Breathable, moisture-wicking liners can be worn alone or as a base layer paired with shell gloves. (Croce & Wir)

HOT-WEATHER CLOTHING

Clothing protects you from heat as well as cold. To remain reasonably cool while climbing a wooded trail in the Smokey Mountains on a hot July day, for example, peel down to your undershirt. At the same time, be prepared for changing weather conditions. A hot, muggy afternoon in mountain terrain can turn quickly into a cold, frosty evening.

Clothing for extreme heat must be loose fitting, moisture wicking, quick-drying, and vented, so the hot air is pumped out during exertion. For the tropics as well as the desert, you'll need high-performance synthetic clothing and cotton for comfort when you're not perspiring too much, preferably long-sleeved shirts and long pants. Wicking T-shirts and shorts are ideal. Your warm-weather clothes should be light colored to reflect the sun.

Again, layering is important even in hot climates. Don't believe me? Consider that in the hot Southwest, temperatures can vary by 50 degrees Fahrenheit on any given day, even within a few hours.

Sun Protection

Clothing plays a large role in preventing sunburn. We've all read the warnings: the sun's UV rays are dangerous. Within just five minutes on a sunny summer day, your skin may absorb enough UV radiation to develop a minor sunburn. And in even less time, your skin cells may suffer injury that you can neither see nor feel. Multiplied over years, the damage from daily sun exposure may lead to skin cancer and sun-induced skin aging. In the past we put on cotton shirts and slathered ourselves with goop to keep these harmful rays at bay, but now we know that a typical T-shirt blocks only 50 percent of the sun's harmful UVA and UVB rays.

Because I am Celt with light skin and blue eyes, I take extra precautions when camping on

In hot, sunny weather, choose lightweight clothes that are quick drying. Long pants are sometimes necessary due to insects and poisonous plants or for sun protection. (Elara Tanguy)

sunny days. Aside from a broad-brimmed hat treated with a sun protective coating and sunscreen, I have also purchased shirts and pants made with Solarknit fabrics. These clothes feel cottony and are lightweight, high wicking, and mildew

Hats are essential for sun protection. (Tula Hats)

resistant while blocking out approximately 95 percent of the sun's harmful UVA and UVB rays.

ACCESSORIES

Bandannas

Okay, bandannas may seem a little dated, but they're practical. This simple piece of material can make a huge difference in your camping experience, regardless of where and what season of the year you

---

DOG CAMPING

For many of us, pets are part of the family. When we go camping, our dog not only assumes he's invited, he's the first one to jump in the car.

Just as camping inspires awe in children, dogs will walk a little faster and open their eyes a little wider as they take in the sights and smells of the new environment.

To make sure your dog is comfortable, consider the following:

- **Bedding:** A blanket, pad, or air mattress will help keep your dog warm, dry, and clean. He'll feel more comfortable in his bed from home. Spread a plastic ground cloth under the bed to keep out moisture. Also, if the dog gets wet, dry him before he enters the tent. The smell of a wet dog is not endearing.
- **Booties:** If your dog is a tenderfoot and you'll be hiking in an area with rocky terrain, bring along dog booties to protect his feet.
- **Water:** Dogs need clean drinking water just like we do. Even if the area you camp in has water all around, it could be contaminated with parasites, harmful bacteria, or chemicals. If the water source is iffy, make sure your dog has clean drinking water just like you do.

Dog panniers should be matched to Fido's body size so he can carry the load. Equally important are proper padding between the dog and pack, and enough ground clearance so he can lie down when the packs are loaded. (RuffWear)

DOG CAMPING (*continued*)

> **Food:** Take plenty of dog food—two days' extra—just in case the open air makes your dog extra hungry. Raccoons, bears, and other wild animals will take an interest in dog food if it's left in the open. Take the same precautions you would with your own food.
>
> If you're backpacking, it's OK to make Fido carry his own supplies. Dog packing is great fun for you and your pooch, as long as his pack is properly fitted and he's not overloaded. Your canine may take to it right away or may need some encouragement and training. Condition your dog to wearing the pack by putting it on him when the two of you are out walking. Start with quick outings and gradually build up to longer hikes. Just remember he's a dog and not a pack mule; you still have to carry your own gear.

are camping. How do you use a bandanna? Let me count the ways: neckerchief, nose rag, keychain, belt, glasses cleaner, washrag, towel, dinner napkin, potholder, sling, flyswatter, sunscreen, and hat. Plus, if you're camping in mosquito country, you can douse your bandanna with insect repellent and wrap it around your neck.

Sunglasses

Sunglasses are not only for summer use. They're just as important in winter, when the sun reflects off the snow, and when the sun's low angle aims its rays right into your eyes even at midday. Look for large-framed, wraparound sunglasses, with polarized lenses and excellent protection against ultraviolet UV radiation.

When shopping for sunglasses, make sure the frames fit. Sunglasses should fit snugly yet rest comfortably on the bridge of your nose and around the ears, and they should not touch your cheeks.

Polarized sunglasses are the only way to cut glare. The Panoptx pictured here come with antifog coating, 100 percent UV protection, a hydrophobic hard coating that repels water, and a removable foam eye seal that comfortably blocks swirling wind and dust. (Panoptx)

Whenever possible, select lightweight frames. If you prefer metal or wire-core frames, you may be able to bend the frames for a better fit. Pay particular attention to fit when buying sunglasses for children. Avoid choosing sunglasses that a child can grow into. Infants might feel comfortable wearing sunglasses made of flexible plastic rather than metal.

Bugs Be Gone

Do you yearn to be swat-free? Clothes that incorporate bug repellent are becoming more and more popular. The Buzz Off Insect Shield used in clothing provides protection against numerous summer pests (ticks, ants, flies, jiggers, and mosquitoes) and has been approved by the Environmental Protection Agency (EPA). The odorless substance, made from an all-natural insect repellent derived from the chrysanthemum plant, is built into everything from jeans and khakis to bandannas and socks. The bug repellent protection is temporary, however; you

QUICK TIP: A THOUSAND WORDS

Be sure to pack a camera and plenty of film or disk space. If you have kids, give each child a disposable camera to record activities and experiences.

can expect it to last through twenty-five or more washes.

KIDS' CLOTHING

All of the advice above applies to children as well as adults, but children have some unique needs.

The main difference is the dirt factor. Kids love dirt, particularly in mud form. Dirt goes hand in hand with camping, so your children's clothing will undoubtedly look scruffy in no time. Forget the high-tech, expensive outfits and dress your youngsters in denim overalls or jeans. Remember to pack a pair of sweatpants; they stretch enough to be worn over jeans on cold days. To minimize packing, plan to let your kids wear the same shirt and pants for consecutive days, but bring a change of socks and underwear for each day. Socks can also serve as mittens on cold mornings.

Some kids insist on wearing pajamas to bed when camping; others are glad for the chance to do something different, such as sleep in a sweatsuit or their underwear. The younger they are, the more worthwhile it is to accommodate their preferences here. Bedtime can be an issue at the best of times, and in an unfamiliar environment it can be doubly unsettling. If space is at a premium, consider packing a pair of ultra-compact PJs that scrunch down to almost nothing.

Pack at least two pairs of shoes: sturdy shoes for hiking, and sandals for the shower. Flip-flops are invaluable at the beach and around the campsite. They can easily be slipped off every time your child enters the tent, preventing dirt and debris from getting into the sleeping area.

Assemble each child's clothing in individual bags. This way they can reach for their outfits in the morning and be set for the day. At night, you can stuff their dirty duds into a separate bag.

Stash some clean clothes in the car for the return trip home. These—along with a damp cloth for the hands and face, plus a hair comb—will

Ultralight clothes such as packable PJs contribute to camping comfort. Cocoon PJs pack into a pouch the size of your palm and weigh less than 4 ounces combined. (Cocoon by Design Salt)

transform your dirty little gnomes into fresh-faced nobility.

CLEANING CAMP CLOTHES

Outdoor clothing—from waterproofed material to base layers—tends to work better when clean. As a general rule, camp clothes should be washed in warm water (86 degrees to 104 degrees Fahrenheit) with mild soap rather than detergent. To remove stains, gently rub the face of the fabric with a soft brush, or consult the care label to see if a stain-removing product can used.

When you're out of range of a coin laundry for a long time, you might try rain-rinsing your clothes. During a downpour, set the clothes on a rock or any clean surface off the ground, and let the rainwater do the work.

FOOTWEAR

Boots

Boots are among the most important pieces of hiking equipment. Heavy boots provide support when carrying large loads and traversing difficult terrain; however, these agonizingly heavy "waffle stompers" are overkill for dayhikers.

There are many types and variations of hiking boots. Finding the right pair requires a little bit of homework. Manufacturers and experts generally agree that hiking boots fall into three main categories: lightweight, backpacking, and mountaineering. Because this book is all about comfort, we'll look at the first two categories, and leave mountaineering boots for the more rugged and adventurous types.

Lose some weight off your feet. For hikes and weekend trips, join the ultralight enthusiasts and opt for lightweight hiking boots or trail shoes. What you choose is related to your pack weight. If you're carrying a light pack, you don't need heavy-duty boots. And, because each pound on your feet

BOOT ANATOMY

The **upper** is the entire upper part of the boot. It should protect the foot with an all-over snug fit, give necessary support, and absorb shocks. The upper of most good-quality boots is leather or a mix of leather and synthetic materials. Ideally, the upper should be waterproof yet breathable.

The **tongue** is the flap that covers the inlet of the upper. Most hiking boots have a gusset connecting the tongue to the upper. The gusset prevents water, dirt, and debris from entering the shoe. Look for a fully gusseted tongue that covers the openings of the upper.

The **midsole**, which contributes to a lot of the boot's weight, does the work of the boot. This part of the boot is responsible for its firmness and weight distribution. The midsole is usually made from ethyl vinyl acetate (EVA), polyurethane, or a combination of both. Although EVA is lighter and softer than polyurethane, it compresses faster and becomes less effective for cushioning. Polyurethane is heavier, firmer, and more durable. Many manufacturers add gel, air cushioning, or bladders and other structures to the midsole to provide maximum cushioning and shock absorption.

The **shank**, which is built into the middle of the midsole, is like a miniature, rigid sole that provides extra stability. Most shank designs start at the heel, go through the arch area, and end just before the ball of the foot where the boot needs to flex.

The **insole** is the bottom part of the inner where your foot rests. A first-rate insole is usually made of plastic and foam. It should be shaped perfectly for your feet, to ensure maximum support and balance. It also corrects some pronation—the tendency many people have to walk on the inside of their feet.

The **outsole** is the part of the boot that contacts the ground. Look for a multi-directional tread pattern, which provides good traction on a wide variety of surfaces and under any conditions. The outsole should absorb and redirect shocks and cushion the soles of your feet. It should be stiff enough to give effective support yet flexible enough to facilitate the natural walking motion of your feet. It should be firmly connected to the upper by stitching or strong adhesives. Double stitching is the method used in better hiking shoes because it's durable and allows for the replacement of another sole once the original is worn down. Cementing is less expensive, but usually less durable.

(continued)

BOOT ANATOMY (*continued*)

pull-on finger tab

upper

tall foam-padded, sewn-in, gusseted tongue

combination of D-rings and speed hooks to adjust laces and fine-tune fit

foam padding around ankle support

combination of nylon and leather upper for light weight and breathability

stabilizing footbed for fine-tuning fit

heel cup (heel counter) for support and stability

protective toe rand

nylon lasting board (insole) for torsional support

molded polyurethane/EVA midsole for shock absorption

high-rubber-content lugged outsole for good traction shank

A basic knowledge of boot anatomy will help you make the best choice for your feet. (Elara Tanguy)

is supposedly equivalent to five pounds on your back, a pair of lighter-weight boots can really lighten your load.

Not all lightweight hiking boots are the same. Let's take a look at some common varieties.

Lightweight boots and trail shoes are usually constructed with all leather or a nylon mesh and leather combination for breathability and comfort. Lightweight hikers are easier to break in and less likely to cause fatigue and blisters than backpacking boots.

Backpacking boots are usually constructed with leather or fabric/leather uppers for durability and water protection. Many also feature a moisture-wicking lining to keep feet dry, and durable rubber lug outsoles for traction. Backpacking boots are more supportive than day-hiking boots.

Shopping for Hiking Boots

When trying on boots, wear the socks you plan to wear on the trail.

To get a good fit, always start with an accurate foot measurement. Feet change size with age, pregnancy, and other weight loss or gain, and even as a result of athletic activity. And manufacturers' sizing varies with each style and pair of boots. So even though you probably know your size, let expert fitters size your feet for the best possible fit. Also, try on boots at the end of the day. Feet tend to swell from morning to night (the gravity thing).

FOOTWEAR TYPE	WEIGHT	BEST USE
Lightweight hikers (light boots/trail shoes)	13 oz. to 2 lbs. 6 oz. $35–$75	Day hiking, short overnight trips
Backpacking boots	3–4 lbs. $100–$190	On-and-off trail hiking on moderate terrain
Trail sandals	1lb. 4 oz to 2 lbs. 5 oz. $55–$95	Hiking and walking in warm conditions. Can be worn with socks in cooler weather.
Casual sandals	4 oz. to 1 lb. 4 oz. $20–$75	Camp shoes for all modes from backpacking to kayak/canoe camping
Water sandals	8 oz.–1 lb. 2 oz. $25–$100	Flexible protection, drainage and cooling for hiking through streams and romping in the surf and other watersport activities
Moccasins	6.6 oz–7.5 oz. $20–$75	Padding around camp or cabin on evenings or weekends. Lessens impact on site
Walking shoes	1lb. 2 oz–1 lb. 6 oz. $40–$70 Race walking $80–$100	Walking from fitness walking to casual strolls
Running shoes	11.8 oz.–1b. 9 oz. $24–$95	Running and jogging
Booties	4.5 oz.–12 oz. $20–$30	Forays beyond confines of sleeping bag

Heat can also make them bigger. You want to make sure the boots will be comfortable with some extra room at all times of the day.

Put your foot into the boot and, before lacing it, push your foot all the way forward. Check to see that the space between your heel and the back of the boot is no more than two fingers and no less than one. Then kick the heel of each boot on the floor to make sure that the heel of your foot is all the way back and seated properly in the boot.

Lightweight hiking boots. (Merrell)

Backpacking boots. (Merrell)

Next, lace up the boots and walk around the store for at least fifteen minutes (the longer, the better). Question the salesperson about any places where the boot does not feel comfortable.

When dealing with mail-order outfitters, be sure to follow their sizing instructions. Most require a pencil outline of your feet (some prefer that you wear socks when making this tracing; others do not.) Test the fit of the boots once you receive them, and ship them back if you are dissatisfied.

Breaking in New Boots

Once you purchase a pair of boots, break them in slowly. It will take about a week. Tackling a mountain right away will doubtless be uncomfortable. If you bought leather boots, take a few dayhikes before embarking on a big trip, or wear them around the house or when you're mowing the lawn. If you have leather boots and you notice any pressure points, apply leather conditioner to those areas to loosen the fit.

Boot Care

Whatever boots you select, treat them properly to get the maximum wear and comfort. Above all, avoid using your boots to rearrange hot coals in a fire ring. Excessive heat of the fire and the alkaline in wood ash will degrade the leather and adhesives.

Condition leather and nylon with Granger's or Nikwax. You should treat your new boots twice when you get them, then once every season to increase their water repellency and make them last longer. Use a silicon-based waterproofing treatment on leather, concentrating on the seams. By the very nature of the holes created when stitching, the seams of stitched boots can become porous over time. Wax-based waterproofing treatments are less desirable because they inhibit breathability.

Sandals

Sandals are still popular despite the fact their design has changed little from antiquity. Any innovation has been in the materials used. In this regard, sandals have come a long way in just the last twenty years.

Trail sandals. (Chris Townsend)

Hiking sandals can take you just about anywhere boots can, but they leave your feet exposed to sharp sticks, jagged rocks, sunburn, and insects.

Water sandals are perfect for any activity involving a lot of time with your feet in the water such as rafting, sea kayaking, or canoeing. They're also comfortable for just hanging out at the beach. The essential feature of water sandals is the all-synthetic materials, which makes them suitable for long-term immersion. Look for a quick-drying nylon upper, a comfortable footbed, and an outsole with strong grip for wet surfaces. Avoid Velcro closures. Velcro works fine for the first half season or so, but eventually, when waterlogged, it loses a substantial amount of stickiness. Buckles are the gold standard for anything worn in the water.

Some sandals (like lovers and spouses) are more supportive than others. Scout around and find a pair that has relatively good support, but pay attention to weight too; you don't want to carry pounds of footwear around with you. Also look for adjustable but solid straps, molded arch support, and shaped footbeds. The outsole should have sufficient tread for rough terrain.

Water sandals. (Chaco)

FIRESIDE FOOTWEAR

Camp booties. (Acorn)

Insulated camp booties keep your feet warmer around camp than your hiking boots. Sometimes you can find booties sold as wet-weather cycling overshoes. Look for styles that are made from fleece-lined rubberized laminate, which keeps water out and heat in.

For simplicity, it's hard to improve on moccasins. There is something sensual and natural about the comfy feel of a well-constructed moccasin; they massage the tired foot as you wiggle your toes.

Flip-flops or casual sandals are also great for a campsite, particularly when standing in grungy campground showers.

Camp moccasins. (Acorn)

Casual sandals. (Chaco)

SOCKS

Wearing new high-tech boots with cheap or worn-out socks is like curling up in a luxurious sleeping bag with no pad underneath. High-end camping socks are expensive, but they're priceless when it comes to reducing blisters. A hiking sock can offer improved cushioning at key points, wick sweat away from your feet, keep your tootsies warm, fine-tune your boot fit, and reduce friction inside the boot.

Modern hiking socks are made from a blend of natural and synthetic materials; these blends provide a good balance of warmth, strength, thickness, and wicking capabilities. If your feet tend to get cold easily, you want wool in the mix. Look for socks made from merino wool, which has softer, finer fibers than regular wool. Silk is another natural fiber commonly found in socks. It wicks moisture and provides a smooth feel. Forget cotton. It bunches up and rubs against your skin, guaranteeing blisters.

For maximum comfort and blister protection, it's best to wear two layers of socks—a thin polyester or silk inner sock paired with a thicker outer sock. The inner layer wicks moisture from the skin, keeping it dry. The outer layer cushions and insulates and also wicks away moisture. Additionally, the liner acts as a second skin, providing additional protection against blisters. It's also a good idea to bring extra socks on the trail: change them often and dry out the ones you've taken off. That way you'll always hike with a warm, dry socks.

CHAPTER 7

COOKING

Everything seems to taste better in the woods—no matter how imperfectly it's cooked. Last summer my son made his specialty, mac 'n' cheese, but it came out in solid scorched lumps. Still, we gobbled it down. The great thing about camp cooking is that if you make a mistake, so what? The culinary police aren't going to bust you. Satirist Jonathan Swift once advised: "If a lump of soot falls into the soup and you cannot conveniently get it out, stir it in well and it will give the soup a French taste." Now there's a man suited to camp cooking.

The point is you don't have to take it too seriously. Never lose sight of the fact that your number-one priority on an outdoor trip should be to have a good time and enjoy nature. Your meals don't have to be extravagant, elaborate, or expensive. With a good cooler, a small camp stove, a grill, and a few utensils, you can cook almost anything you would cook at home. All it takes to become an outdoor chef is a little planning and ingenuity.

Today, camp cooks have more options than ever before in terms of food and equipment; however, just like clothing and gear, certain food items and cooking gear aren't perfect for every trip. Items that are too heavy for backpacking trips, might be perfect for car camping, while menus that are perfect for backpacking might be too spartan for an RVer. Before you shop for food and equipment, ask yourself some simple questions:

▶ *How many days will you be camping?*
▶ *How many people will you be feeding?*
▶ *Does anybody in the group have special dietary needs?*
▶ *Are there foods that everybody likes to eat?*
▶ *Will kids be part of the group?*
▶ *How much cooking do you want to do?*

Most importantly, what type of camping will you be doing?

Spices can save a bland camp meal. You can make your own portable spice kit or buy one at an outfitter. My favorite kit is the GSI Outdoors Waterproof Spicer, which holds six different seasonings in its break-resistant containers.

The GSI Outdoors Spicer. (GSI Outdoors)

COOKING SUPPLIES FOR CAR CAMPERS AND RVERS

Camping from your vehicle can allow you to eat just as well as you would from home. To do so, however, you'll need the right tools. If you're a traveling gourmet, portable refrigeration should top your list.

Keeping Food Cold

Camping provides unique challenges in maintaining food safety. Eggs, meat, poultry, fish, milk, some fresh produce, and precooked foods need to be stored at temperatures below or close to 40 degrees. During extended trips, it is especially difficult to keep the food as cold as necessary. Nowadays, there

are two solutions: coolers—the old standby—and portable electric refrigerators.

Regardless of what kind of cooler you get, keeping it out of the sun will go along way toward preserving its contents. Car trunks tend to get pretty hot during summer travel; instead, keep your cooler on the backseat of your car—with the air-conditioning on. Add extra insulation by wrapping the cooler in a beach towel or a blanket. Keep the cooler in the shade at the campsite, too.

Ice Coolers

Ice coolers come in two varieties, hard-sided and soft-sided.

When shopping for a hard-sided ice cooler, make certain it's well insulated with a tight-fitting lid and is spacious enough for your needs. Some hard-sided coolers have wheels that allow you to roll your food from the car to the campsite.

Soft-sided coolers are lighter than hard-sided coolers, easier to carry, more compact (they can be collapsed when empty), and less expensive. They don't insulate as well as hard-sided coolers, however.

When filling the cooler, keep in mind that block ice lasts much longer than cubes. On the other hand, packing food items in a bed of ice cubes tends to preserve food better. If you have room, consider using both cubes and an ice block. If space is limited, use large frozen steaks or containers of frozen juice as cooling blocks. Toward the end of your trip, the frozen items will have thawed and they'll be ready to eat.

Electric Coolers

New thermoelectric coolers plug into your vehicle's cigarette lighter and keep things chilled—without ice—while you're on the road. Thermoelectric coolers will keep your food and drinks about 40 degrees cooler than the outside temperature.

Some thermoelectric coolers have adaptors that allow you to plug them into standard wall outlets.

Coleman's 50-quart Ultimate Xtreme Cooler will keep ice for six days in 90-degree temperatures—about twice as long as conventional coolers of the same size. (The Coleman Company, Inc.)

Thermoelectric cooler. (The Coleman Company, Inc.)

This is a handy feature if your campsite has an electricity hookup.

Propane Refrigerators

Propane refrigerators aren't that common, but they have advantages. Lofty Shelters manufactures a wheeled camping fridge that boasts a three-way operation. It runs on 120 volts when loading at home, 12 volts when plugged in the cigarette lighter in the car, and on a propane canister when camping.

Cooking Gear

If you're RVing, you'll do most of your cooking inside the vehicle, enjoying the convenience of a

SNACKS

Snacks are often overlooked in the food planning, so stock up big in this department. Good snack foods for all campers include:

▶ trail mix (your favorite mixture of dried fruits, nuts, and seeds)
▶ granola
▶ fruit leather
▶ wasabi peas
▶ sesame sticks
▶ fresh fruit, for variety

Avoid energy bars or other snacks that contain a lot of chocolate. Chocolate melts and can get messy. Hot chocolate mix satisfies your chocolate craving without making a mess. You can make hot chocolate or lick it out of the packet—as I have been known to do.

full kitchen with running water, stovetop, oven, microwave, toaster, dishwasher, et cetera. Car campers have a variety of choices when it comes to cooking. The most common option is the camp stove.

Camp Stoves

Modern camp stoves are remarkably compact, lightweight, efficient, and easy to use, with features such as a push-button ignition, flame control adjustment, self-cleaning fuel jets, and ample burner space. Even kitchen klutzes like me can whip up a delicate soufflé or a hearty stew, a stack of buckwheat pancakes, or a crepe on these modern stoves. What's more, there's a wider range of fuel than ever before: propane, butane, kerosene, white gasoline, and even unleaded gas. (See Fuel Comparisons on page 89.)

Suitcase stoves have two or three burners. No matter what type of stove you bring, make sure you

pack sufficient fuel for your trip, or you may end up eating cold food right from the package.

Most car campers opt for two- and three-burner suitcase stoves. These stoves resemble an attaché case, complete with carrying handle. The top folds back to reveal the burners, and a wing unfolds from each side of the top to create a windbreak. You connect the fuel container to the stove and, presto, you're ready to cook.

The benefits of a suitcase stove are obvious. Two or three burners allow you to prepare more dishes simultaneously, and the large burners do a better job of heating foods evenly. Most big stoves are very stable, with wide, sturdy grates over the burners, to support heavy pots of food.

The Brunton Wind River Range, for example, is a professional-grade two-burner stove that holds up well in the field. It's compatible with large or small propane canisters, and will run for 1$\frac{1}{2}$ hours at high output (15,000 btu's per burner) on a

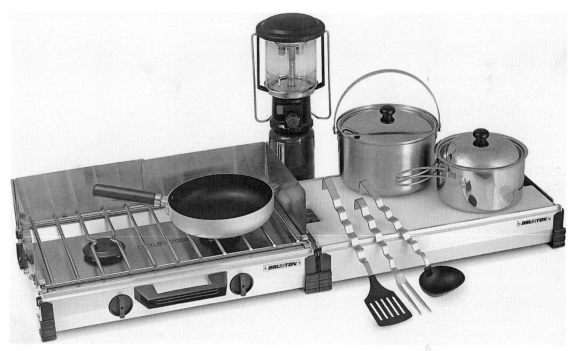

Two-burner stove. (Brunton)

PORTABLE FURNITURE

Camping used to mean sitting on rocks and preparing food on logs, but now you can pack furniture with you.

Camping is more comfortable if you have a lightweight, compact chair. The Trekker Chair allows you to convert a Therm-a-Rest self-inflating camp mattress into a comfortable seat. (Therm-a-Rest)

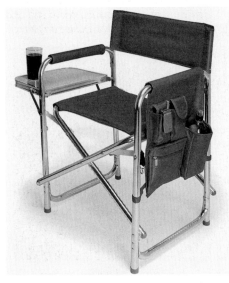

The Crazy Legs leisure chair has a swiveling table that can be used as a regular table or swiveled around in front of you to hold your drink, dinner, book, or computer. The table height and tilt are adjustable. (Crazy Creek)

The lightweight aluminum Trail Sling is just the ticket for weight-shaving backpackers. It reduces down to the size of tent poles, then unfolds to become a comfortable off-the-ground chair with good back support and a padded headrest. (GCI Outdoor)

A homemade chuck box provides compact storage for camp cookware and gives you a clean work space for food preparation. Cabela's Chuck Box can be ordered fully stocked with utensils and tableware. The work surface serves as a cutting board and also has room for a two-burner stove. (Jonathan Hanson)

Not all campsites have a picnic table. Here's a sturdy full-height table that sets up in minutes for eating yet packs easily for storage and portability. (Picnic Time)

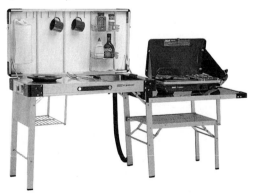

A portable camp kitchen makes food preparation more fun. Features can include a sink, pantry, hanging rack, and cutting board. This kitchen helps keep the picnic table clear for other activities, such as playing cards. (The Coleman Company, Inc.)

A dining fly is a practical addition to any camp. It can be in front of the tent or it can stand alone to provide shade and comfort while you cook, eat, and clean up. In a pinch, use an old tarp tied between trees. (Johnson Outdoors, Inc.)

single fuel canister. Coleman's Fold 'n Go stove is more economical and easy to transport. Although it has two 15,000-btu burners plus a heavy-gauge steel wire grill, it's still 25 percent more compact than a traditional two-burner camp stove.

Camp Slow Cooker

A propane slow cooker is a welcome addition to the camp kitchen for on-the-go cooks like me. I just add the ingredients for soups, stews, chili, et cetera, and this gadget slow cooks them, which enhances the flavors, then it maintains a warm temperature when the cooking is done.

Camp Oven

Another convenient addition to the camp kitchen is a propane oven, with its consistent heat and a view glass. It enables you to bake your favorite foods in camp. Just make sure to bring along oven mitts, because the exterior surface of a propane oven gets hot.

Portable Fire Rings

Portable fire rings are ideal for camping. Arctic's portable fire ring includes a porcelain-coated

QUICK TIP: KEEP IT TOGETHER

Make sure that everything is *in* something—a pack, a plastic tub, a cardboard box, or some other container—and keep similar objects together. For example, you might put all breakfast foods into one sack, lunch in another, and dinner into a third.

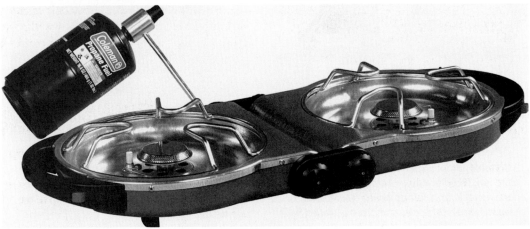

The Fold 'n Go stove. (The Coleman Company, Inc.)

Coleman's Road Heat 'n Serve slow cooker liberates meal preparation from a wall socket. Each propane cylinder keeps food warm for five hours on high and up to ten hours on low. (The Coleman Company, Inc.)

Propane oven. (The Coleman Company, Inc.)

cast-iron cooking grid that adjusts to three different heights and swivels. A 12-inch heavy-duty cast-iron outer ring keeps your log fire under control.

Griddles

Griddles can be used over a campfire, although cooking on them requires hot coals rather than flames. Griddles also work especially well on a two-burner camp stove, where the heat can be controlled more easily.

CAMPFIRE COOKING

When all else fails, you can always cook the old fashioned way—by campfire. To build a campfire, you'll need tinder, kindling, and logs. Tinder is anything that ignites with a spark or a match, such as paper or dry grass. Kindling is small pieces of wood such as twigs and thin branches that burn quickly and easily and help to ignite logs.

Use the existing fire rings at your campsite and, during dry seasons, make sure there are no fire restrictions.

Dutch oven. (Left: GSI, Right: Alan S. Kesselheim)

Dutch Ovens

If I had to venture into the woods with just one cooking utensil, it would be a Dutch oven. It's been an old reliable for some time. When Lewis and Clark made their pioneering trek to the Northwest in 1805, they listed the Dutch oven as one of their most valued pieces of equipment. Versatility is what makes it such an essential kitchen item: it can be used for nearly every type of cooking.

The traditional Dutch oven is a heavy cast-iron kettle with a flat bottom, three short legs, and a tight-fitting lipped lid with a handle in the center. Like all cast-iron cookware, a Dutch oven works best when it is allowed to season with prolonged use.

Position your Dutch oven over a bed of briquettes or coals, place more of them on the lid, and, presto, the food inside cooks as it would in an actual oven. When preparing dishes with a high

COFFEE

Coffee rituals come in many guises but never fail to elicit intense opinions. Until recently, before coffee became a stylish addiction, the standard was "cowboy coffee": you simply dumped ground coffee beans into a pot of boiling water. But now the options have expanded. You can get your wilderness coffee fix from a mini-espresso maker, or a premeasured one-cup coffee "teabag," or a drip-style coffeemaker. Use any of these to brew a "cuppa joe" just like you do at home.

Drip coffeemaker. (The Coleman Company, Inc.)

Reflector oven. (Sproul's of Maine)

liquid content, such as stews and soups, place two-thirds of the coals beneath the pot and one-third on top. When baking, reverse the proportions: one-third beneath and two-thirds on top.

Reflector Ovens

A reflector oven is a shiny aluminum "half box" with a shelf in the middle to support the food being baked. A metal bar or rear legs support the shelf and keep it horizontal. A reflector oven is almost as versatile as a Dutch oven but is easier to use, because a flaming fire rather than coals are required.

Heat radiating from the fire strikes the sloping walls of the oven and is reflected up and down to the food. You can build your campfire high, with lots of flames, which is a plus on a cold night. Also, you can see the food while it bakes, so it's easy to adjust the cooking time and temperature as needed. Simply move the oven to control the heat.

Aluminum Foil

Foil is the easiest and cheapest camp cooking you can find. All you need is a roll of heavy-duty aluminum foil and a campfire. Simply wrap food in a piece of foil and fold over the edges so the steam can't escape.

Potatoes are a natural for foil cooking. Wrap 'em up and place them in the center of hot coals. Cooking can vary from 25 to 45 minutes depending on size of potatoes and heat of fire. Check for doneness with a fork. The utensil should pull out of the potato without sticking.

When cooking meats and fish, seal packages so there's little or no space between the foil and the food. Close contact between food, foil, and fire helps brown the food. When cooking vegetables and other foods, however, it may be preferable to "tent" the foil over the food. The extra air space allows the package to act like a pressure cooker, steaming the food until it is done without browning it. You might add a few ice cubes to aluminum foil dinners or vegetable packets to prevent them from burning and to keep them moist.

After cooking, carefully open the end of the packet to allow the steam to escape before opening the top of the packet.

Cookware

Your choice of cookware depends on your method of cooking. Grilling requires tongs, skewers, and a grill, for example, whereas stovetop cooking may require only a fork, spoon, and spatula.

New campers often make the mistake of bringing household utensils into camp, only to find that they are not suitable. After a few weeks they're in

DON'T FORGET THE S'MORES

Kids love and expect s'mores on every camping trip. This ultimate fireside creation has been around since 1927 when the recipe first appeared in the Girl Scout guide to camping. All you need is graham crackers, marshmallows, chocolate bars, and a campfire. Put a marshmallow on a stick and hold it over a flame. For perfect results, the marshmallows must be hot enough to melt the chocolate between the graham crackers to make a sandwich.

PACKING TIPS

Sometimes your eyes are bigger than your trunk or backpack. Make sure that all camping items will fit into your cooler, car, and backpack *before* the morning of your departure. Here are some pointers:

▸ **Access:** When packing your car, arrange the equipment so that you can easily get at your cooler. This way, when you stop at a grocery store you can add food and ice without having to unload gear.
▸ **Organization:** Keep the food and cooking gear in separate containers. Avoid unwieldy

storage boxes: not only are they too heavy to lug from car to camp, the larger the storage box, the more stuff you'll have to shift around to get what you need. Small but sturdy plastic containers, such as those made by Rubbermaid, are ideal.

▸ **Packaging:** Cut down on bulk by repackaging items in ziplock bags. (Be sure to label the contents and include cooking directions.) Also, keep related items together: pack the spaghetti with the sauce, and measure out powdered milk and store it with pancake mix.

rough shape. Aluminum cookware gets dented, wooden handles get charred over open flames, and glassware cracks or breaks. Instead, look for cookware made from these materials:

▸ **Stainless steel** *is tough, easy to clean, and noncorroding. If there's any downside, it's the extra weight.*
▸ **Titanium** *is super lightweight and extremely tough but costs more than other options and conducts heat less evenly than stainless steel.*
▸ **Cast iron** *is ideal for fixed-camp or cabin use. It is heavy duty and more durable and retains heat longer than other options.*
▸ **Enamelware** *(the familiar blue, green, and white pots) is durable and has a fire-resistant finish, but it is heavy.*

SUPPLIES FOR BACKPACKERS, PADDLERS, AND CYCLISTS

Hikers, bikers, and paddlers have fewer options when it comes to food and cookware. No reasonable backpacker, for instance, is going to pack a

cast-iron skillet, a three-burner camp stove, or a half-pound of ground chuck. Space, weight, and lack of refrigeration are big issues for those who venture beyond the campgrounds. Thankfully, there are many products to meet their demands.

Backpacker Stoves

Backpacker stoves are compact and weigh only a few ounces. They have evolved in recent years, and

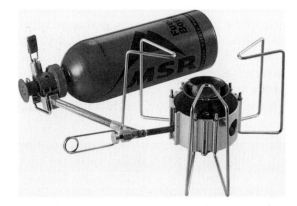

The fold-out supports on this backpacker stove make it a stable surface for large, heavy pots—a smart choice for group campers. The DragonFly burns any fuel, including white gas, diesel, automotive, and jet fuel. (MSR)

Backpackers don't have to sacrifice all luxuries. The GSI MiniEspresso is designed for use on low heat over a backpacking stove. The tank holds 3 ounces of water and ground coffee. Makes a cup in ninety seconds. (GSI Outdoors)

The Coleman Exponent backpacker table, which adjusts to fit most trees, includes gear hooks that hold up to 50 pounds altogether; the table itself holds 25 pounds, weighs 20 ounces, and rolls up to fit in a backpack. (The Coleman Company, Inc.)

many now offer features similar to those on larger suitcase stoves, including push-button ignition and a wide range of fuel choices. Small size is a strength and a weakness, however. Backpacker stoves can be a bit unstable, particularly when supporting large, heavy pots. Plus, a small burner often produces a hot spot on the pan rather than diffusing the heat evenly across the bottom of the pan. For these reasons, look for stoves with fold-out pot supports. Also, look for heat-diffuser plates; they capture heat from the stove and disperse it evenly, preventing hot spots.

WASHING UP

The best cooks are also the cleanest, but, for campers, that's easier said than done. If you're lucky, your campground will have sinks where you can wash pots and dishes. If not, here are some tips:

▸ Clean as you go. You don't want to scrub by flashlight, so keep the cooking station clean as you prepare meals.

▸ Heat a pan of water over the fire while you eat so you'll have hot water ready for cleanup when you are done.
▸ Use a biodegradable detergent.
▸ Cowboys scoured pans with sand and gravel. Lucky for you, a simple plastic or metal scouring pad will serve just as well.

Lightweight Foods

Modern freeze-dried foods are a godsend. They are flash-frozen, then placed in a vacuum chamber where moisture is removed, cutting their weight by more than 70 percent. Freeze-dried foods have greatly simplified backcountry cooking while also broadening the palette. Nowadays it's common to serve chicken pad thai, curried vegetables, or fettuccini alfredo in deep wilderness. Preparation is beyond easy. Boil a few cups of water, pour it into one of the meal pouches, close the zipper seal, wait five minutes, then open and eat. The best part of all? You don't need to dirty any dishes; just eat them straight out of the bag. I find the freeze-dried meals to be delicious and use them often. (In fact, in a pinch I've served them to guests at home.) Three brands I prefer are Backpacker's Pantry, Cache Lake, and Alpine Aire.

Freeze-dried foods are conveniently packaged in one-, two-, four-, and six-person portions, weigh mere ounces, require no refrigeration, and last up to two years unopened without spoilage.

The biggest drawback to freeze-dried foods is cost. They are expensive. Still, when you consider that there is no waste and much of the preparation has been done for you, the convenience is well worth the extra expense, especially when you need to travel light and have no means of refrigeration.

If freeze-dried food seems too costly, consider dehydrated food. It is not frozen but merely dried by any number of methods. Boil-in-the-bag rice, for instance, is easy, cooks up fast, and cleans up easily; it is well worth the few extra cents per serving that it costs over rice prepared from scratch. Other just-add-water foods such as soups, chili, and cups of noodles are ideal no-cleanup meals and snacks. These foods are found in most supermarkets.

If you're ambitious and enjoy food preparation, try home-drying your food. Many cookbooks are likely to contain a chapter on drying food. Dehydrating is a good bet for sauces, thick soups, fruits,

Freeze-dried food is appetizing, easy to fix, and lightweight. Just make sure that the amount of food you buy will be adequate for the campers in your group. (Chris Townsend)

A food dehydrator saves you money and space. It lets you do food prep ahead of time, reducing tasty dishes such as beans and rice, chili, pastas, and soups to compact, lightweight ziplock packets. (Adrienne Hall)

and vegetables. If you'll be doing a lot of dehydrating, consider buying a multi-tray food dehydrator.

FUEL COMPARISONS

Whether you're a car camper or a backpacker, you'll need to consider fuels when shopping for camp stoves. Not all fuels are equal, and there are many tradeoffs when considering price, availability, weight, and heat output.

Camp stoves generally accept fuel from one of two possible sources: 1) refillable tanks that use liquid fuel; or 2) disposable canisters that are filled with highly pressurized fuel.

In all cases, be sure to read the manufacturer's instructions carefully before igniting your stove.

Refillable Tanks

There are many different kinds of liquid gas options for refillable fuel tanks. Some liquid-fuel stoves are designed to burn more than one type of fuel, which gives the user some flexibility if the primary fuel is unavailable; however, don't try to burn a fuel for which the stove is not designed.

White Gas

The most common liquid camp fuel by far is white gas (commonly referred to as Coleman fuel). White gas is sold in gallon-size cans; some liquid-fuel stoves have a special fitting that allows you to connect the can directly to the stove, but most require you to pour the white gas into its refillable tank. Either way, the fuel tank must be pressurized (with a small built-in pump) before you can light the stove. Large flames may occur when the stove is first lit. They can be alarming to some people, and can present a fire hazard, but the flames will subside once the stove heats up.

Disposable Canisters

Disposable canisters are filled with either propane, butane, or a mixture of both. Stoves

COOKING TIPS

▶ Cook once, eat twice—or more. Leftover meats are tomorrow's sandwiches and omelettes; leftover grilled vegetables are delicious in camp scrambles.
▶ Choose quick-cooking items to save fuel.
▶ Scrambled eggs go further if you add breadcrumbs.

▶ Stew dried fruits during dinner preparations so they'll be ready for breakfast.
▶ Cover pots when cooking. Food will cook more quickly, and you will save on fuel. Also, lids help keep dirt and insects out of food.

that use canisters are generally lighter, plus they're easier to maintain because the fuel burns cleaner.

Propane canisters are relatively heavy, so they are most often seen with suitcase stoves, where size and weight have already been sacrificed to convenience and ease of use. Butane and butane-propane blends are sold in smaller, lighter canisters, which are more commonly used with smaller

backpacking stoves, although some suitcase stoves use them as well.

Stoves that use disposable canisters are usually more expensive than their refillable counterparts. They don't burn as hot, but they can be regulated better for a low flame. Some canisters are recyclable, but most are meant to be discarded when empty. Of course, empties *must* be packed out and disposed of appropriately.

FUEL TYPES COMPARED

FUEL	COST	PROS	CONS	BEST USE
Propane	Expensive	Clean burning Efficient No priming required Instant maximum heat output	Cartridge disposal an environmental concern Lower heat output than white gas or kerosene Greater fuel bulk	Campground camping
Butane	Expensive	Convenient Relatively lightweight Works well at high elevations Can be adjusted for simmering	Sold only in disposable cartridges Difficulty vaporizing in cold weather (although mixing with propane enhances performance)	All types of camping at temperatures above 40 degrees F
White gas	Inexpensive	Efficient and reliable Works well in cold weather and at high elevations	Requires priming Prone to flare-ups Environmental hazard if spilled into lakes and streams	Backpacking Group camping Cold-weather camping
Kerosene	Inexpensive	Readily available High heat output	Burns dirty and smelly Messy to handle Blackens pots Can clog stove parts	Camping in areas where other fuels are unavailable
Alcohol	Inexpensive	Stores well Burns silently Low volatility	Burns only half as hot as other fuels Requires longer cooking time	Camping in areas where other fuels are unavailable
Unleaded auto gas	Inexpensive	Can be found virtually anywhere	Dirty, sooty, and volatile; use only when necessary	Camping in areas where other fuels are unavailable

CHAPTER 8

BICYCLE CAMPING

A bike is the ideal vehicle for breezing through the countryside taking in the scenery. If the whim hits to duck off on a side trip to explore a riverbank or take in a small-town museum, what's to stop you?

Pedaling a fully loaded bicycle can be quite difficult at times, but it's cake next to the burden a backpacker carries. Aside from that obvious difference, bicycle camping can allow for a great deal of comfort. For one thing, cyclists are rarely

TOURING OPTIONS FOR THE BICYCLER

▶ **Supported touring**. A support-and-gear van, or SAG van, carries your food and gear from one overnight stop to the next. You carry just enough gear to get you through the day.

▶ **Self-guided tours**. Many companies offer tour packages that include lodging, luggage transfers, route planning, meals, and rental bikes. The company does all the logistics planning; you simply follow the route. Groups can also get together and organize their own self-guided tours perhaps with vehicle support provided by a friend.

▶ **Credit-card tours**. Perhaps the most liberating (and expensive) form of bike touring involves just you, your bike, and a credit card in your back pocket. You eat and sleep at whatever location strikes you.

▶ **Bicycle camping**. So-called loaded touring is just what it sounds like: you carry everything with you (food, cooking equipment, tent, sleeping bag, clothes, and personal gear).

For touring information and suggestions, consult the Adventure Cycling Association (www.adv-cycling.org) and the National Bicycle Tour Director's Association (www.nbtda.com).

far from civilization, so, in the event of bad weather, you can simply skip the tent for a night and stay in a motel. Yes, there will be hot or rainy spells and times when you'll have to quit riding and repair your bike, but these problems are usually infrequent and easily dealt with, whereas the sheer pleasure of the trip remains in your mind for years.

Bicycle camping requires a lot of expensive gear (bike, packs, camping supplies). Before you go shopping, equip yourself with information.

■

BIKES

The key to comfortable bicycle camping is to go light. By giving careful consideration to your choice of bike and equipment, you can pack for extended tours yet still avoid heavy loads.

Fortunately, today's bikes are lighter and more dependable than ever. Components have become more reliable, additional gears make climbing less arduous, and stronger brakes provide excellent downhill control.

The best bicycle for travel is a touring bike. These packhorses are not built for speed; rather they are designed to shoulder the weight of your gear while providing comfort and reliability. Their wide tires are suitable for unpaved roads but they're faster than the fat tires used on mountain bikes.

A touring bike's wheel base (the distance between the front and back wheels) is longer than other bikes, which makes for greater straight-line stability; however, this also results in slower turns. Nonetheless, higher stability equals greater comfort—especially when traveling long distances.

A touring bike's frame is longer and lower than most bikes. The long frame helps to accommodate gear, and the low center of gravity adds to the overall stability. The low frame also results in a lower seat height, making the bike easier to mount and dismount.

Bike Fitting and Adjusting

A bike that's too big or too small will be uncomfortable and handle poorly, and it can be a safety hazard. A bad fit can trigger a numb rear end, burning feet, knee or back pain, sore hands, achy shoulders,

Touring bike. (Ortlieb)

and a stiff neck. On the other hand, a correct fit will make even a cheap frame ride better, and a high-quality frame function like an extension of your body.

Frame

When being fitted for a bike, first look at frame size by straddling the top tube. The top tube is the horizontal part of the frame between the handlebars and the seat. There should be 1 to 2 inches of clearance between the top tube and your crotch. If you're buying a hybrid bike for mixed road and off-road touring, you should have 3 to 4 four inches of clearance.

Reach

Next, assess the reach—the distance between the seat and the handlebars. When you sit on the seat, you should be able to comfortably grip the handlebars. If the handlebars are too far away, you won't have adequate control; if they're too close, you'll be uncomfortable and tire easily. There are four factors that affect the reach on a bike: 1) the top tube; 2) the stem; 3) the handlebars; and 4) the seat.

The top tube is a deal breaker because it can't be adjusted. If the top tube is not the right fit, look for another bike.

The stem connects the handlebars to the front fork. Some stems clamp the handlebars almost directly above the head tube—the part of the frame that holds the stem and the fork. Other stems hold the handlebars well forward of the head tube. If the frame is the right size but the reach is still too long, consider replacing the stem for one with shorter forward extension.

The handlebars can affect the reach in several different ways. Handlebars come in many shapes: some force you to lean farther down and forward than others. The style of bar also influences the type of brake levers that are attached to it and where they're mounted. You want your hands to be on or near the brakes at all times. And the bars can be angled up or down in the clamp on top of the stem, which will also influence how straight you can sit up or how far down you must bend your torso. Luckily, you can adjust or simply replace handlebars for a better fit. (Also, be sure

to check the width of the handlebars from proper fit. Put your hands on the handlebars in your regular riding position; your hands should be at about the same width as your shoulders.)

The seat post can be raised or lowered in the frame, and the seat itself can be slid backward or forward in its clamp atop the seat post. Try adjusting the seat position to attain the proper reach. Also, the type of seat will affect your whole posture, which, in turn, will affect how far you can comfortably reach.

Seat

Seats affect more than just reach, however. Seat height is a critical issue for comfort and efficiency. Most people tend to adjust their seat too low, which prevents them from extending their legs far enough to make use of the most powerful muscles, so they tire faster than necessary. On the other hand, if the seat is too high, you'll have to shift your torso from side to side for every stroke of the pedals. This imposes a whole raft of problems, including wasted energy, bike control difficulties, chafe between your legs, and possible long-term orthopedic issues.

The correct seat height allows your heel to just barely press against the pedal when your leg is fully extended at the bottom of the stroke. When making this adjustment, be sure your body remains straight on the bike's centerline. If this seems like too much guesswork, go to a bike shop. A good shop will have special equipment to precisely measure your body and make the appropriate adjustment.

The angle of the seat is equally critical. In general, it's best to have the seat level, although some people are more comfortable with a very slight forward tilt. Never set the seat more than 3 degrees from horizontal.

The fore-and-aft position of the seat determines how you are balanced on the bike between the seat and the handlebars. Too far forward places excessive weight on the seat, while too far back places excessive weight on the handlebars.

Long-term comfort on the bike is determined by a balance of factors. Leaning forward reduces wind resistance, which means easier pedaling, but it puts more weight on your arms and wrists than a more upright position, and it may bother your back. Many people find a well-padded saddle more comfortable to sit on, but it can rob you of some of your pedaling efficiency and may chafe you in a sensitive area. On the other hand, few bicycle tourers find hard, unpadded, racing-style saddles at all comfortable, even though they do contribute to efficiency.

How to Shop for a Bike

When it's time to buy a bike, a bike shop is usually your best bet. Discount stores give you a bike in a box, or pay someone who isn't knowledgeable about bicycles to assemble it for you. What usually happens is that some of the bearings are not adjusted properly. They are often shipped too tight from the factory and, if not adjusted, will grind themselves up in no time. In almost all cases, discount store bikes are heavier, although they are considerably less expensive.

Even if you'll be putting yourself in the hands of the salesperson, it's a good idea to learn as much as you can about bicycle design. You increase your chances of getting a better deal if you demonstrate a real interest in bicycles. You will notice that most people who work in bike shops do so because they love cycling and get a real kick out of talking about bikes and giving advice.

Veteran tourers sometimes prefer to buy their bike on the Internet or at a custom bike shop. They know exactly what they want, and a local bike shop might not be able to meet their needs. They've had extensive experience with different sizes of bikes and they've got frame sizing down to a science. Novices who buy a bike on the Internet, however, will have to assemble it themselves or hire someone to do so (and many shops will be reluctant to set up a brand-new bike that they didn't sell you). Before you take off, make sure:

▶ *tires are fully inflated*
▶ *brakes and gears are adjusted properly and you know how to use them*
▶ *seat is properly adjusted*

Before going to the bike store, make sure you are wearing comfortable cycling clothes which means they aren't binding or constrictive. Bring along your toe clips and helmet for the road test. Request that the salesman watch you for a bit. As you try out the bike, concentrate on your ability to reach the brakes. The "reach" should be within your arm's reach. Though you will most likely be limited to the area around the bike store, get up enough speed to know if you can pedal the bike efficiently and safely. Ask yourself if the bike is a good fit for your physical and riding style; that is, machine and body working in sync. Is the bike a pleasure to ride? Go with the bike that's most comfortable for you.

Choosing Bike Components

Sometimes you find the perfect bike; other times you make it. You may fall in love with a particular bike's frame, derailleurs, brakes, and crankset yet feel ambivalent toward the seat, handlebars, and tires. Some shops will gladly swap components as part of the sale, and you'll have to pay only the difference between the existing part and the custom replacement. Other shops may only be willing to sell you the bike as is, then sell you additional parts. (On the plus side, the shop will probably install it for you at no extra charge if it's part of a new-bike sale.)

Handlebars
Touring bikes are usually equipped with drop-style handlebars—the familiar racing-style bars that curve forward, down, then back. Drop-style handlebars offer numerous grip positions, which allow you to vary your riding stance throughout the day. Varying your stance can reduce stiffness, muscle fatigue, or numbness. Drop-style handlebars also allow you to ride in a crouched position which greatly reduces wind resistance. Drop handlebars are covered with plastic, leather, or cloth tape to ensure a good grip and to provide a more comfortable surface than the bare metal of the bar itself.

Flat handlebars, like those usually fitted to mountain bikes, provide very firm control, which is

Flat handlebars. (Dahon)

essential over rough terrain. You hold onto rubbery handgrips at the ends of the bars. The more upright riding position of flat bars also offers better vision, and many people find it more comfortable. Those who tour with flat bars often add curved extensions to provide additional riding positions.

Seat

Your relationship with the saddle is an intimate one, to say the least. A seat should feel good and give adequate support without interfering with your riding position. Manufacturers often skimp on

Drop-style handlebars. (Kestrel)

Wide seats are the heaviest. They are wide throughout, especially at the back, and come with lots of padding. If the saddle is too wide, however, it is likely to cause chafing. (Planet Bike)

seats—even on expensive bikes—so be prepared to pay for an upgrade.

Finding the seat that's right for you will require considerable bottoms-on research. In your quest for the Holy Grail of bike seats, you'll encounter many different kinds:

▶ **Comfort saddles** *are wide and well padded. They're easy on the rear in the short term, but they lower performance and can chafe.*
▶ **Racing seats** *favor lightness and stiffness for maximum pedaling efficiency at the expense of comfort and support.*
▶ **Ergonomically designed seats** *can prevent discomfort, but they don't necessarily lend themselves to efficient pedaling.*
▶ **Leather seats** *are strong and durable and mold to your bottom, but they require more care than synthetics.*
▶ **Synthetic leather seats are** *less expensive and usually more waterproof than genuine leather seats, but some cyclists think they are less comfortable than leather.*
▶ **Synthetic padded and gel-filled seats** *are pliable but not particularly durable. I've gone through several and wouldn't buy another.*

Ergonomic seat. (Planet Bike)

Pedal Clips

For efficient riding, you have to fasten your foot to the pedal, either with toe clips or by using so-called clipless pedals. Both systems keep your feet in the optimum position for efficient pedaling, so you're powering on the upstroke as well as the down. This means less ankle and knee pressure and less muscle fatigue.

Toe clips are metal or plastic cages attached to the front of the pedal into which you slip your foot as soon as you gain some forward motion. You then tighten a strap enough to keep your foot in

Clipless pedals. (Bebop, Inc.)

place, yet not so tight that you can't free your foot for a quick dismount.

Clipless pedals are designed to lock onto a cleat that you mount to the soles of your riding shoes. (The pedals and cleats are sold as a set.) To lock in, you simply step down on the pedal. To release, you just twist your heel out to the side. Clipless pedals are easier to use than toe clips, but the cleat renders the shoes useless for anything besides biking. This means you'll need to pack an extra set of shoes on every trip.

Many new riders are reluctant to try either of these systems. The idea of your feet being locked to the pedals seems dangerous, but it's not. Give them a shot and you'll soon realize how safe and efficient they are.

Tires

High-quality tires are essential. Most bikes come from the factory with adequate tires, but not necessarily the ones you want.

On smooth pavement, wide tires are slower and skinny tires are faster; however, the wider ones— $1\frac{1}{2}$ inches (38 millimeters)—are better for bike touring. Skinny tires produce a pounding ride on rough pavement, are more prone to flats, and aren't good on gravel roads. Tires should be somewhat soft to provide a less-harsh ride, but not below the recommended minimum inflation pressure. Learn how to fix flats, and keep a patch kit, an extra inner tube, and a folding spare tire with you when you tour.

Fenders

Some cyclists ride without fenders in all weather conditions; other riders would never be caught without them. As far as comfort goes, a bike with

Toe clips. (Delta Cycle Corp, www.deltacycle.com)

ASK AN EXPERT

Richard A. Lovett, author of *The Essential Touring Cyclist*, took a few moments to field some gear questions.

Q: What's your favorite tent?

A: My favorite tent is a Eureka Zephyr, which probably is no longer made. It's a one-person, free-standing tent that weighs roughly 3 pounds, has a very narrow footprint, and is just tall enough to sit up in. A free-standing tent frees me to camp anywhere in my western locale, even in spots where there's often no chance of driving in stakes. The narrowness of the tent also helps, allowing it to fit between rocks, or sagebushes, or whatever else might force bigger tents into other areas.

Q: What's your favorite sleeping bag?

A: I don't have a favorite sleeping bag. As an Oregonian, I'm not fond of down. If it gets wet, you're in big trouble, and while I like deserts I also like places like Iceland, where "wet" is very much an issue. I have multiple sleeping bags of different weights, depending on conditions. I'm also fond of bivvy bags. You can use these, even car camping, to stretch a 3-season tent/bag into colder temperatures. (They give you an extra 5–10 degrees of comfort zone in the tent.) You can also use them outside the tent, to sleep under the stars. On a bicycle, they're a lot easier to pack than a tent, since they fit in a pannier, and are a lot lighter. They are not, however, good places to weather a long storm . . . or a mosquito attack, or anything else. Basically they're to shut off breezes at night and keep you dry in a pinch. They also let you star gaze.

In short, I'd go for something made of fast-drying synthetic fill that's still compressible. Keeping the weight reasonable also helps.

Q: What's your favorite sleeping pad?

A: I'm a fan of Therm-a-Rest, though the REI versions are probably the same. A relatively thin pad blown up really firm works fine—probably better than a slightly thicker but softer one. That allows it to bridge underlying lumps, like rocks, and tree roots. Get a stuff sack that fits the pad, and set aside the sack that the pad is sold with. Their original sacks presume you can fold the pad into in the same super-tight bundle the factory did. I use a long, thin stuff sack I bought somewhere. A sack is important because if you snag the pad on something you'll hole the stuff sack not the pad.

Q: What's your favorite stove?

A: This one's simple: the MSR Pocket Rocket. It's light, reliable, produces a super-intense flame that boils water quickly. Most of all, I like it because it's legal on an airplane (as of this writing). The Pocket Rocket is nothing more than a nozzle that screws into the MSR propane fuel bottles (beware of other brands; the threads might not match). Fly with just the rocket, then buy fuel at your destination.

There is one major disadvantage. The thing is basically a propane torch. You have to be careful that it's on a flat surface so it doesn't get knocked over. Caution is advised; the prospect for serious burns exists.

Q: What gear innovation of the past 10 years or so makes the biggest difference in comfort for your sport?

A: Improved anatomical saddles. It used to be that it took a few weeks each spring to break in your posterior to a new season's riding. These days, I never worry about that. Anatomical saddles started to appear 10 years ago, but it's only been relatively recently that I've had a seat that really, truly meant no problems.

(continued)

> **Q:** **In your opinion, which oft-recommended items of gear are unnecessary?**
>
> **A:** Anything that smacks of the Tour de France. Bicycling equipment is strongly driven by racing, and you can spend enormous amounts of money equipping yourself like Lance Armstrong. If you're out there to smell the roses, however, a 1 or 2 percent speed gain hardly matters. And if you're going to carry a handlebar bag with a camera and assorted supplies, a super-nimble, multi-thousand-dollar bicycle would be a waste. You also don't want the expensive, paper-thin racing tires, because they go flat all the time.
>
> Also beware of anything that's touted to be "the latest, greatest innovation." Bicycle touring takes you to small towns in the middle of nowhere; if your latest-greatest gear breaks down, you don't want the local bike mechanic saying, "What the heck is *that?*"

fenders is better than one without. Road spray is a problem if you lack fenders; the front tire will throw mud and rain water at your face while the rear tire will shower your back. Fenders do, however, add weight and create wind resistance.

Most touring bikes are sold without fenders. If you plan to add them, make sure the bike has mounting points on the front and rear forks.

Bike Tools and Maintenance

Flat tires, broken spokes, and countless other problems come with the territory of bike touring. Luckily, bikes aren't hard to fix. Their construction is simple, and the parts are right there in front of you. With homework and practice, you'll learn to troubleshoot mechanical problems on the road. Just

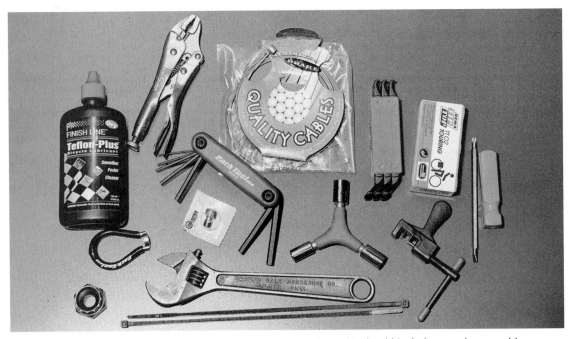

Keep your tool kit handy under your seat or in your pannier. A basic kit should include wrench, screwdriver, spare tube, patches for tube and tires, air pump, and pliers. (Vera Jagendorf)

make sure you have the proper tools and know how to use them. Before embarking on a camping trip, you should know how to fix a flat tire, a broken chain, and make minor adjustments to your derailleur.

CARRYING YOUR GEAR

Traveling long distances with gear on your bike is not a job for your backpack. Wearing a heavy backpack while riding would be tremendously uncomfortable and, more significantly, would raise your center of gravity so high as to make the bike unstable.

There are two practical options. You can carry your gear in panniers—bags that mount on special racks—or you can tow your gear in a trailer. Each has its conveniences and drawbacks.

If you're determined to carry all the comforts of home and you have the leg muscles to do it, you could tow a trailer *and* mount front panniers on your bike.

Racks and Panniers

Racks can be mounted on bicycles to hold panniers. Racks come in two types, front and rear. Most people start with rear racks. Some folks eventually add front racks, which allow them to carry more stuff and balance out the load on the bike a little better.

Avoid buying cheap racks. To comfortably carry large loads such as camping gear, you need sturdy racks. Aluminum-manganese alloy racks are extremely strong, lightweight, and rigid. They should be bolted with self-locking nuts to fittings on the bike frame. Rack mountings need regular checking and tightening, especially during the early stages of a camping trip and over rocky terrain.

Panniers are usually made of a synthetic waterproof material and have a hooded lid for

Front panniers (top) and rear panniers for touring. Zippered outside pockets allow easy access to essential items. (Trudy E. Bell [top]; Delta Cycle Corp, www.deltacycle.com [bottom])

added protection. They are usually sold in sets and hook onto the upper rails of the rack and also attach to points near the axles. Panniers make it easy to organize your belongings: many have both

PANNIERS VERSUS TRAILERS

PRICE	PROS	CONS	BEST USE
PANNIERS			
$130–$250	Durable Make for easy gear organizing	Front panniers increase wind resistance Add direct weight to bike Challenging to pack with even weight distribution	More stability for cyclists who like speed
TRAILERS			
$399	Can carry more weight, such as bulky gear Weight is kept low to the ground	Add to handling challenges while turning on variable terrain Two-wheeled variety increases wind and rolling resistance Gear less accessible Difficult to park	Camping with lots of gear on established trails and roads

interior and exterior pockets for tools and other frequently needed items.

It's important that panniers fasten firmly to the rack and don't sway when the bike leans. Make sure they cannot come into contact with the spokes, and check to see that you have sufficient

clearance between your heels and the front of the rear panniers.

Trailers

Trailers come in a variety of styles and sizes and have multiple uses, such as hauling gear and pulling kids. Some have one wheel, some have two.

Trailers weigh between 17 and 20 pounds; adding 40 to 50 pounds of gear can cause braking and handling problems, although probably no more than what occur when you load the weight right onto the bike itself, as with panniers. The width of the trailer can also be an issue if you plan to ride narrow trails. The extra weight, rolling friction, and wind resistance of a trailer can make hills and headwinds more of a problem.

But trailers allow you to carry more weight and larger objects than do panniers. With so much gear capacity, however, you have to beware of overpacking.

WATER

Stay hydrated! Be sure to outfit your bike with bottle cages. Bottle cages attach to your bike's frame and can hold plastic water bottles. Some cyclists prefer to carry water in a hydration pack such as a Camelback.

Bottle cage. (Delta Cycle Corp, www.deltacycle.com)

Handlebar Bags and Seat Pouches

Once you've decided on your bike and your primary gear-carrying equipment, you might be able to talk

BOB Trailer (for Beast of Burden) is a packhorse with an open frame. It is equipped with rear reflectors and a safety flag. (BOB Trailers, Inc.)

the bike shop into throwing some smaller equipment into the deal, such as handlebar bags or a seat pouch.

Handlebar bags provide easy access to things like money, snacks, or a camera. Many have a convenient see-through map case on the top flap so you can check your route while riding. When you dismount, the bags can be easily removed and slung over your shoulder.

Quality handlebar bags come with a rack that attaches to the handlebars for stability; some also have an inner frame, which makes the bag more solid. Cheaper bags use only straps as a suspension device, which may allow the bag to sway or otherwise interfere with your front brakes or cables. Unless you really need the extra space, it's best to choose a small model and fill it only partially, because handlebar bags rest high on your steering column and can affect steering and balance.

Seat pouches attach to the underside of your bike seat, behind the seat post, where they create minimal wind resistance. They have a very limited capacity but are a good place to stash tire-repair tools.

CLOTHING AND SAFETY GEAR

Being comfortable means dressing the part. General-purpose outerwear isn't designed for the cyclist's posture and range of movements, so it often feels constricting. Also, cycling clothes are generally more aerodynamic than your average outfit. Invest in some good cycling clothes and your body will thank you after a day in the saddle.

For bicycle camping, you'll want bright-colored clothing so you're highly visible to traffic, but you don't need to go overboard. This isn't the Tour de France.

Helmets

In the old days, helmets were stuffy and uncomfortable; today, helmets are lighter, they provide excellent ventilation, and they provide better protection. Not all helmets are right for you, however.

A properly fitted helmet will pay big dividends in both safety and comfort.

You want a helmet that makes contact with your head all the way around. It should be level and stable enough to resist movement even if it's struck or shaken. It should be as low on the head as possible to maximize side coverage, and the strap should fit snugly.

Helmets that fit with foam pads come with at least one set of pads. Buying a second set of thicker pads allows you to customize the shape. For starters, you can often remove the top pad entirely or substitute the thinnest ones. This lowers the helmet on the head, bringing its protection down further on the sides.

Some helmets use a fitting ring rather than side pads; these helmets are not usually as comfortable as the ones with pads. Loosening the ring can produce a sloppy fit.

Gloves

Cycling gloves may strike you as a luxury, but they are actually important for safety and comfort. Gloves keep your hands warm in cool weather, and ensure a secure grip to the handlebars. More importantly, gloves can cushion the blow if you hit the deck.

Whether you choose full-finger or half-finger gloves, be sure that the palms are well padded. The pads will protect the nerves in your hands and fingers from the numbing vibrations of road cycling.

Also look for good breathability and moisture absorption.

Sunglasses

Cyclists often ride for hours in the glaring sun. Sunglasses are essential to comfort and safety; they improve vision and protect your eyes from wind, bugs, and sharp pebbles thrown into the air by passing vehicles. They are essential for any biker who has sensitive eyes or wears contact lenses.

You might want to try cycling sunglasses with interchangeable lenses—dark lenses for sunny conditions, yellow lenses for overcast days when more contrast is needed, and clear lenses when light is at a premium.

Shorts and Pants

If your posterior—like mine—is less than perfect, you might shy away from wearing cycling shorts or pants. Well, get over it! No article of clothing will have more impact on your comfort than these funny-looking skintight garments. Cycling subjects your most sensitive areas to cruel and unusual punishment. Long days over rough ground—particularly in hot or tropical climates—results in an uncomfortable mixture of moisture and friction—a recipe for rashes and chafing.

Spandex cycling shorts and pants are made to absorb moisture and reduce chafing. Cycling shorts are worn next to the skin and provide a seam-free and comfortable garment. If you're still feeling shy, you can always wear a looser-fitting pair of shorts over your cycling shorts, but you might not have the same seam-free experience.

Jerseys and Jackets

Clothing for the upper body is far less critical for the cyclist than pants. Low wind resistance and adequate protection are the only criteria that need to be met. Cycling jerseys are designed to meet these requirements. Most are made of moisture-wicking fabrics to keep you cooler in warm weather and warmer in cool weather. They are usually cut with a longer tail for better coverage of your back while you're in the riding position, and feature zippers for ventilation. (Avoid cotton fabrics; they retain moisture, which can weigh down the rider and cause chills.)

Rain Gear

Wearing the right gear can make all the difference in wet conditions. Rain gear for cycling keeps water out, but it often locks moisture in. Fortunately, many rain suits have full-length zippers to vent perspiration.

I prefer cycling in a poncho during wet weather. It's completely open at the bottom, thus allowing air to circulate around the body while still shedding rain.

Rain suits made with high-tech fabrics such as Gore-Tex and incorporating features such as vents that allow air in but keep water out can add to your comfort.

———■———

PACKING

Whether using panniers or a trailer, you need to strike a balance between comfort and manageable weight. Touring cyclists are notorious for their weight consciousness, to the extent of cutting handles off toothbrushes and throwing away books or using them for toilet paper as soon as they have finished reading them. On the other hand, bikers have the luxury of carrying more weight than backpackers, so you can afford to pack a few luxuries if you wish.

With either system, it's important to work out an efficient approach to packing. A bicycle is more stable if the pack weight (panniers or trailer) is low and evenly distributed. Distribute weight evenly from side to side, and pack the heaviest items as low as possible. If you're using panniers, more weight will inevitably be in the rear, because the rear panniers are larger, but make sure that some of your heavier gear is up front to avoid being *too* rear-heavy. Too much weight in the rear can cause the bike to shimmy uncomfortably while braking.

Bike tourers must decide on their objectives: a strenuous workout, a leisurely ride, a night in the wilderness, or a stay at a comfortable resort. (Richard A. Lovett)

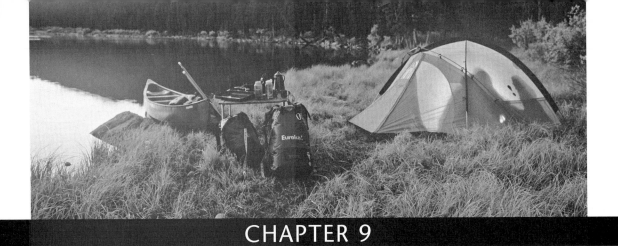

CHAPTER 9

BOAT CAMPING

Is there any better way to see, smell, and feel nature up close than from a kayak or a canoe? These simple vessels can take you to hidden coves, tidal salt marshes, or along rocky shores—places that larger motorized craft can't go. Plus, by slicing quietly through the water, you can sneak up on wildlife in their natural habitat.

Kayak and canoe camping are probably two of the easiest camping adventures you can experience. They are relaxing, gentle sports where the efficiency of the stroke, not the power of it, is what's important. All you need is a stable boat, safety gear, navigational aids, and reliable camping equipment. And, because weight and volume is less of an issue, you can pack a few luxury items that would incapacitate backpackers.

Of course, a kayaking or canoe trip isn't all serenity. Buck a headwind all day or portage a fully loaded boat and you'll feel pain in muscles you didn't know you had.

KAYAKS VS. CANOES

Kayaks and canoes are very similar in many respects. Both can be transported on top of a car or in the back of a truck, and most people can carry either one without assistance. Both are easy to learn and, even if mistakes happen, both are virtually unsinkable.

Despite these many similarities, however, kayaks and canoes each have distinct pros and cons.

Kayaks

A kayak has a lower profile than a canoe and, therefore, is less affected by headwinds and crosswinds. Its narrow hull slips through the water more easily than a canoe's, making it nimbler and faster.

A kayak is a relatively small boat, but it can store a lot of gear. (Doug Hayward)

Sealed compartments, or bulkheads, at the front and back of many kayaks form airtight chambers; if a kayak capsizes, only the cockpit portion of the kayak will flood.

It's easier to keep a kayak moving in a straight line because your double-ended blade allows you to paddle on alternating sides, plus your hips and legs press against the sides of the kayak, which allow your body to help steer.

Kayaks are not without some drawbacks, however. Kayaks can be expensive—especially when you consider that you'll need one kayak per person. (Tandem kayaks are available but they're much

rarer and more expensive.) Also, kayaks often feel less stable than canoes.

Canoes

The late Canadian filmmaker Bill Mason called the canoe "the simplest, most functional, yet aesthetically pleasing object ever created," and legions of families would certainly agree. With stability and lots of space, a canoe offers paddling comfort for parents and kids. Whereas a family of four would have to buy four kayaks, a canoe can hold mom on one end, dad on the other, and two

DESIGN CONSIDERATIONS

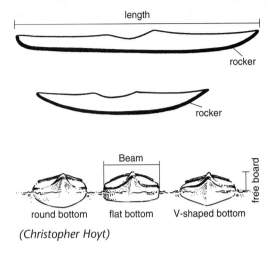

length

rocker

rocker

Beam

free board

round bottom   flat bottom   V-shaped bottom

(Christopher Hoyt)

Whether comparing canoes or kayaks, it is possible to make general assumptions about each boat's performance and comfort by simply looking at its length, beam, freeboard, rocker, and the shape of its underside.

Length influences a boat's speed. In general, longer boats are faster and, once you get them up to speed, they are easier to paddle over distances. Longer boats also stay on course better, but they are more difficult to maneuver than shorter ones.

Boats with a wide **beam** (the boat's widest point) are more stable but less maneuverable.

Freeboard is the height of a boat's side above the waterline. Higher sides mean you can load more into the boat without swamping it, but they also present more surface area to wind and can be blown off course. If you plan to carry only moderate quantities of gear, select a boat with moderate freeboard.

Look at a boat from the side, and notice the profile of the bottom. If a boat curves upward significantly at its ends, it has a lot of **rocker**; it will be very maneuverable but will not track well. Boats with little rocker hold their direction better, but of course this makes it more difficult to maneuver around rocks in a tightly twisting river.

The shape of a boat's **bottom** affects stability. A flat bottom is more stable in calm water, whereas a rounded bottom works better in rough water. A V-shaped bottom holds a straighter line when paddled.

small kids in the middle. Cost alone is a huge advantage. Canoes are easy to pack and they're generally more stable.

If you capsize, however, the whole boat is going to fill with water and any gear that's not strapped down could float away. Canoes can be a little less responsive when turning and feel sluggish compared to kayaks.

In the end, however, there's no wrong answer. The choice between a kayak and canoe is simply a matter of preference. Before you settle on one you need to experience both. Many outfitters offer demonstration days which give you a chance to try out many boats of both types in a single day. Many stores rent boats by the day or week. This is an excellent way to sample boat camping without committing to a big purchase.

■

KAYAKS

Most touring kayaks have a deck that covers the hull and a hole in the deck called the cockpit, where you sit. The covered area under the deck provides lots of stowage space. Often, the cockpit is divided from the front and back of the kayak by watertight partitions, called bulkheads. Hatches are fitted on the front and rear decks to provide access to the storage spaces fore and aft.

MATERIALS

Plastic boats are the least expensive, the heaviest, and the most durable. You can crash a plastic boat against a rock or drag it along the ground without doing much harm. But when a plastic boat *is* damaged, it can be difficult or impossible to repair.

Fiberglass boats are more expensive than plastic ones but are significantly lighter, which makes them easier to carry and easier to paddle. If, however, you hit a rock or bottom out, you could easily damage the hull. Luckily, repairs to fiberglass are relatively easy.

Expensive materials such as Kevlar and graphite are lighter, yet stronger than fiberglass. The low weight of composite boats makes them easier to paddle and portage than any other type, but they are more difficult to repair than fiberglass.

Aluminum is used for canoes, not kayaks. Aluminum is strong, abrasion resistant, and inexpensive, but it's moderately heavy and poor on comfort. The metal will freeze your fingertips on cold mornings and blister your hands on sweltering afternoons. It tends to

drag and hang up on rocks rather than slipping over them. Aluminum is also "noisy." Every time you hit the side of the canoe with your paddle, you and the fish will hear the bang.

Folding boats, known as fabric-on-frame construction, consist of wooden or aluminum frames covered with a waterproof fabric skin. The skin can be removed and the frames disassembled and everything packed into a bag or two, allowing the boats to be carried in a car trunk, stored in a closet, and checked as airline baggage for travel anywhere in the world. They are less rugged than other materials and, with a few exceptions, tend to be pricey. Their interior framework cuts into their carrying capacity and, in kayaks, can make loading somewhat difficult.

Two other choices are not good options for camping. Canoes and kayaks made of wood, although lovely, are usually custom built, relatively delicate, and tend to be very expensive unless you build them yourself. Most inflatable kayaks, although highly portable, don't have the carrying capacity for comfortable camping.

Aside from these general similarities, however, there are a number of sizes and shapes to choose from.

Types of Kayaks

Light Touring Kayaks

Light touring kayaks are typically 12 to 14 feet long and 22 to 24 inches wide. They have enough

capacity for short overnight trips, but most have no hatches, so gear must be pushed into the ends by way of the cockpit.

Touring Kayaks

Touring kayaks are usually 14 to 16 feet long, 22 to 24 inches wide, and can carry enough gear for a few days. They usually have two hatches that

THE WRONG KAYAKS FOR THE JOB

There are three kinds of kayaks that are *not* appropriate for boat camping. Recreational kayaks are usually about 8 to 10 feet long—too small to carry enough gear for camping and too slow for extended travel. Sit-on-top kayaks

are glorified surfboards and have very little, if any, storage space. Finally, whitewater kayaks are too small with too much rocker. They have neither the gear capacity nor the tracking for boat camping.

Light touring kayaks, including folding kayaks, are built for stability and speed. (Jonathan Hanson)

Touring kayaks are designed for day trips as well as extended expeditions. (Jonathan Hanson)

provide access to sealed storage compartments fore and aft.

Sea Kayaks

Sea kayaks are usually 16 to 18 feet long and 19 to 23 inches wide (tandems can be as long as 22 feet and 36 inches wide). Sea kayaks are capable of sustained high-speed paddling and handling rough offshore conditions, but the kayak may feel "tippy" and require more skill to handle than a touring kayak. On the plus side, you can carry enough gear for a week or more.

Fit and Features

Everyone is built differently and every kayak fits everyone differently. A heavyset paddler may find it difficult to enjoy a 21-inch-wide sea kayak because it is too confining. By the same token, if you're 5 feet 1 inch tall and weigh 125 pounds, a large cockpit will feel too roomy, and you'll be slipping around too much inside it to maneuver the boat well. You can pad any boat for comfort, but ideally it should fit well to begin with. After all, it's often said that paddlers "wear" their kayaks.

Fit and comfort are the primary concerns when shopping for a kayak, but don't overlook these important considerations.

Capacity

Boat manufacturers determine the maximum capacity for each of their vessels. The maximum capacity is the amount of weight a boat can safely carry. It's important to note, however, that a boat loaded to its maximum capacity isn't exactly sprightly on the water. When purchasing a boat, be sure the maximum capacity is higher than you need. On the other hand, an underloaded boat is difficult to control in high winds. Consider how often you'll be paddling with a full camping load versus paddling virtually empty on day trips.

Cockpit Size and Shape

Determine how easily you can enter and exit the boat. A long cockpit and a high deck allow you to sit down in the seat, then pull in your legs, as well

Sea kayaks have enough storage capacity to supply a few weeks of camping. (Doug Hayward)

as to exit legs first. A smaller cockpit requires you to enter feet first and exit butt first, which many paddlers find tricky and uncomfortable.

Backrests

There are many different styles of backrests. Be sure yours is comfortable or you'll spend lots of time at the chiropractor's.

Seats

Seats should hold you in place securely and feel comfortable. Again, you can add padding, but it's best to have a seat that feels good to begin with.

Deck Rigging

Shock cords fastened to the deck are known as deck rigging. They're convenient for holding items you'll want close at hand (such as maps, snacks, water bottles, sunscreen, and a camera).

Rudder

On many longer kayaks, you'll have the option of adding a rudder. Some paddlers say that a good kayaker doesn't need a rudder, and a beginner shouldn't learn to rely on one; however, we're more interested in comfort here. A rudder makes holding a course and turning a kayak easier. It is mounted on the kayak's stern and it's steered with foot levers inside the cockpit.

Skeg

A skeg is like a fin on the underside of a surfboard. A skeg on the kayak's centerline makes it easier to hold the boat on a straight course, especially in high winds; however, skegs also inhibit maneuverability. For this reason, skegs are retractable. Pull on a cable and the skeg is retracted into the hull.

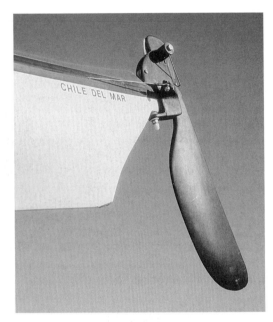

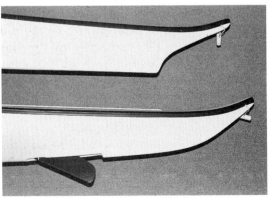

Rudders (top) and skegs (bottom) are devices that can give you greater control. (Jonathan Hanson)

Essential Gear for Kayaks

Personal Flotation Device (PFD)

Any life vest is better than no life vest, but kayakers should be a little discerning. Between the cockpit opening, the backrest, and your spray skirt (see below), you won't have a lot of room to accommodate an oversized PFD, so avoid the $8 orange "horse collar" and buy one specifically designed for kayaking. It's far more comfortable, and safer too. Do *not* paddle without wearing it. Ever!

Paddle

You'll be making thousands of paddle strokes over the course of a day, so the lighter the paddle, the better. Wood or fiberglass shafts are more comfortable to hold than aluminum ones. Wide blades are better for acceleration and sharp maneuvers, but they also present more surface area to the wind, so narrower paddles are preferable in wind-prone areas. One-piece paddles are stronger and lighter; two-piece, or break-apart paddles are more convenient, because they fit in your trunk, and they allow you to change the angle of the blades relative to each other (feathering). Some new paddles allow you to adjust the angle in small increments so you can choose which angle feels best for you.

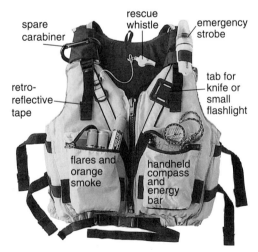

Kayaking PFD. (Doug Hayward)

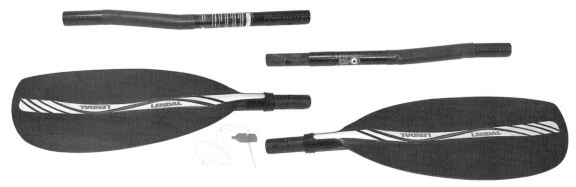

Micro-adjustable paddle. (Lendal Paddles)

Paddle Float

In the event of a capsize, a paddle float can help save the day. Ideally, an Eskimo roll will get you upright with the least amount of fuss or exposure to water; however, it takes practice. If rolling the boat upright is out of the question, you'll have to make what's called a wet exit out of the boat. Once outside, it can be very difficult to get back into a kayak. Here's where a paddle float comes into play. A paddle float is a foam or inflatable sleeve that you pull over one of the paddle's blades. Next, secure the other end of the paddle to the kayak deck such that the paddle extends perpendicularly from the boat to form a makeshift outrigger. Now the boat should be stable enough to crawl back into the cockpit.

Paddle float. (Doug Hayward)

Paddles should be comfortable to hold, and be strong and light enough to withstand many hours of use. A spare paddle should always be carried by kayakers venturing out on the water. (Doug Hayward)

Paddle Leash

If you lose your kayak paddle you'll be, um, lost without a paddle. A paddle leash is a simple cord that fastens your paddle to the boat and prevents you from losing it whenever you reach for a water bottle, use your camera, or apply sunscreen.

Spray Skirt

A spray skirt prevents the hull from taking on water in rough weather or during a roll. The skirt fits around your waist and is attached to the rim of the cockpit to create a watertight seal. Neoprene rubber skirts are the most effective at keeping water out, but they're uncomfortable in hot weather and are more difficult to fasten than nylon skirts.

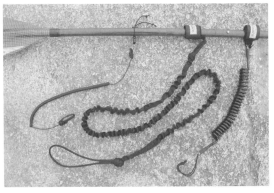

An assortment of paddle leashes. (Doug Hayward)

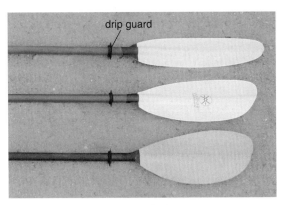

Drip guards. (Doug Hayward)

Drip Guards

Drip guards prevent a form of water torture. These rubber protrusions on the paddle shaft prevent water from running down the shaft and onto your hands and spray skirt every time you alternate strokes.

Float Bags

Flotation bags are designed to keep clothing and gear dry during your paddle. The watertight bags are made of vinyl or coated nylon, and, as the name suggests, they float.

Spray skirt. (Doug Hayward)

Bilge Pump

Either a handheld or deck-mounted bilge pump will help empty your boat if you take on water.

Deck Bag

A deck bag is like a glove compartment in that it holds small items (camera, snacks, charts) within arms' reach. Deck bags are watertight and they are gernerally secured to the deck with bungees.

Deck bag. (Jonathan Hanson)

ASK AN EXPERT

Jonathan Hanson—a sea kayaking instructor and guide, and author of *Complete Sea Kayak Touring*—took a few moments to field questions on his favorite gear.

Q: What's your favorite tent?

A: Once my old Marmot Taku finally gave up the ghost, I bought a Sierra Designs Hercules for solo camping. For trips with my wife, we opted for a North Face VE25. When I choose a tent, the chief criteria is storm resistance. I loathe cheap tents that collapse in wind and leak in rain.

Q: What's your favorite sleeping bag?

A: My Marmot Gore-Tex Grouse. It's a 25-year-old semi-rectangular down bag that is still going strong. It's good to near-freezing; perfect for Baja. For Arctic paddling, I'd opt for a Marmot Snow Goose. Some people argue that you should choose a synthetic bag for sea kayaking because it will keep you warm even if you get it wet; however, if you store it properly, there's no reason why you can't bring a down bag.

Q: What's your favorite sleeping pad?

A: When camping on the desert coastline of Baja, I go with an open-cell foam pad. (It's immune to thorn punctures.)

Q: What's your favorite stove?

The Snow Peak Gigapower. It's supremely compact and lightweight. I can carry an entire spare stove and still not notice the weight or space.

Q: What's the most important clothing and footwear consideration for a kayak camper?

A: Dress for the water temperature; not the air. When the air is 70 degrees and the water is 40 degrees, you need to dress with the assumption that you'll be dunked in that 40-degree water and might even wind up swimming in it for an extended period of time. On my feet I prefer water shoes that can get wet, but still provide enough support and traction for brief shore hikes. I'm not a fan of sandals around the rocky desert coasts I frequent.

Q: What gear innovation of the past 10 years or so makes the biggest difference in comfort for your sport?

A: The carbon-fiber paddle. Taking six ounces off your paddle is like taking a pound off a pair of boots for hiking. It's weight you don't have to constantly lift.

Q: In your opinion, which oft-recommended items of gear are unnecessary?

One item that I've found mostly worthless is an emergency whistle. The sound simply doesn't carry in the conditions you're most likely to need it. A compact air horn is better for noisemaking.

CANOES

Most canoes that you'll see in the shops are appropriate for camping, although some are better than others. You're unlikely to find special-purpose canoes, such as those intended for racing or serious whitewater, unless you seek them out. The only other type you might see (and should stay away from) is meant primarily for fishing. These are short and wide and too slow for long-distance touring.

Although most of the canoes that you see will do the job, canoes that are specifically designed for camping are fast and stable and have lots of carrying capacity.

Types of Canoes

Expedition Canoes

The biggest canoes are called expedition canoes, cruisers, or trippers. They are usually 17 to 18 feet long and they often have as much as 15 inches of freeboard, which gives them a huge gear capacity but also makes them difficult to handle in windy conditions. In general, their size impedes maneuverability.

Expedition canoe. (Doug Hayward)

Touring Canoes

Touring canoes and general-purpose canoes are more common than expedition canoes. They're 16 to 17 feet long, with roughly 13 inches of freeboard. This makes them more maneuverable and less susceptible to wind, but also limits their capacity.

Features

Seats

Most canoes have two seats, although some larger ones have three. When kids are aboard, however, it's often better to put a cushion in the bottom of the boat and have them sit on that. Their weight will be low and less likely to cause a capsize.

A touring canoe. (Johnson Outdoors, Inc.)

I'm partial to woven cane seats; they're flexible and durable, and water can't pool on them, which keeps your bottom dry and comfortable. Solid plastic seats are durable but uncomfortable, and they hold water. A third option is nylon webbing, which has the flexibility and self-draining capability of cane and even better durability, although some paddlers feel that it's not as attractive.

Gunwales

Gunwales (pronounced "gunnels") are the side rails that run along the top edges of the canoe. Plastic and aluminum gunwales require no maintenance. Bare aluminum is lightest, but it can cause glare and is arguably the least attractive. Wood gunwales—made of mahogany, spruce, oak, or ash—are more attractive, but they're heavier and require periodic maintenance.

Thwarts

Thwarts are the transverse braces from gunwale to gunwale. If you plan on portaging your canoe, the center thwart should be shaped like an ox bow; this will allow you to comfortably carry the boat upside-down on your shoulders. Pads can be added

to the center thwart for even more comfort. If the center thwart isn't designed for portaging, make sure the canoe has comfortable handles at the bow and stern for a two-person portage.

Essential Gear for Canoes

PFD

Canoeists can choose from a wider range of PFDs than kayakers, but you should still choose something that fits well and is rated for your weight. Again, a PFD won't do you any good if you're not wearing it.

Paddle

The person in the stern (rear) usually uses a longer paddle than the person in the bow. Try a lot of paddles until you find one where the grip and the shaft feel comfortable. When you consider how many paddle strokes you'll make in the course of a day, weight is an obvious concern. High-tech composites have reduced the weight of paddles to just a few ounces, but they can be somewhat delicate. For that reason, make sure you carry at least one spare paddle in the boat. You may prefer the feel of real wood, but

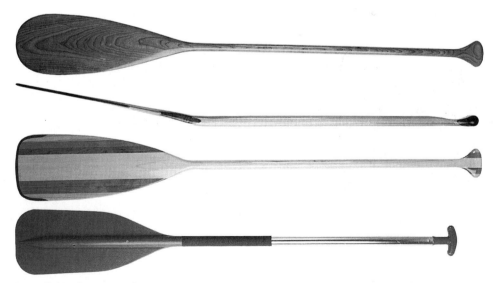

Beautiful and strong, a beavertail (top) has a long narrow blade and a rounded tip. A bent-shaft blade is angled to increase power and efficiency. A straight shaft is good for quick maneuvering, particularly in white water. A t-handle (bottom) provides precision and control.

Seat back. (GCI Outdoor)

it comes at a sacrifice of weight. Cheap aluminum and plastic paddles are good for spares and for white-water rock bashing but not for all-day comfort.

Seat Backs

Seat backs can be fastened to canoe seats to provide lumbar support. They come in various designs, from a plastic grid that clips onto the seat to folding pads that are strapped in place and serve as both seat backs and seat cushions. The latter fold down when they're not needed or can be removed from the canoe and used as camp chairs.

Thwart Bags

Watertight thwart bags can be attached to the canoe and used to keep a camera, snacks, maps, or other small items) handy and out of any bilgewater.

Painter

A rope attached to the bow and/or stern of a boat that is called a painter. A painter can be used to tie the boat to a tree when you come ashore, or to pull the canoe through shallow water. Use a sturdy piece of nylon or Dacron line about 15 to 20 feet long for each painter. Carry bungee cords to coil the painters when they're not in use, to prevent them from trailing in the water or becoming tangled.

WHAT TO BRING

The beauty of canoe camping—and kayak camping to a lesser extent—is that you can bring lots of stuff with you. Kayaks can easily carry two to three

Thwart bag. (Granite Gear)

times as much gear as a backpack, and canoeists can measure their loads in hundreds of pounds. Unless you plan to portage some distance, you can afford to bring some luxuries such as fresh fruit and vegetables, collapsible chairs, maybe even some beer.

Of course, with more room to carry gear, there's a temptation to carry too much. Be forewarned: a heavy boat is a sluggish boat.

Camping Gear

Start with a good synthetic-filled sleeping bag and a self-inflating mattress. There's no need to squeeze yourself into a micro-size, ultralight tent; bring a good-size dome with plenty of stretching-out room. You could bring a string hammock strictly for relaxing. And you could bring along a tent hammock with a rainfly and mosquito-net walls as an alternate to a tent in case you find yourself in a marginal campsite with no good place to pitch a tent.

You'll also have plenty of room for a two-burner propane stove. If you won't be staying in

The GCI Outdoor Top Shelf portable table is a durable camp table that comes in handy if your campsite lacks a picnic table. It has an 18-inch by 18-inch top with a place to attach a garbage bag. (GCI Outdoor)

established campsites with fire rings but want to build campfires anyway, first—before leaving home—make sure they're permitted. If they are, bring a fire pan—a metal pan with high sides to contain the fire and ashes. This will reduce damage to the surrounding vegetation and soil.

Unless you have major portages to contend with, by all means bring folding chairs. If you won't be at campsites with a picnic table, consider bringing a folding or roll-up camp table. GCI Outdoors has a nifty small table with a place on its side to attach a refuse bag.

Canoeists can bring large rigid coolers; kayakers are usually limited to soft-sided small ones. If your cooler doesn't have a latching lid, strap or tie it closed to keep the goods safe inside in case of a capsize.

You'll need some kind of light. The traditional Coleman lantern, which burns white gas, is bulky and noisy, and the mantles are delicate. Instead, consider some of the newer options, which include battery-powered lanterns, and models that burn propane or butane. Of course, only the battery-powered type should ever be brought into a tent. For directional light, many campers prefer headlamps, which leave the hands free for cooking and other tasks.

Clothing and Footwear

The optimal clothing for kayaking and canoeing is loose, quick-drying apparel that feels comfortable, doesn't bind when you're sitting, and doesn't restrict your torso movement. Be prudent and include insulating clothing even when the forecast is for mild weather. There is something heavenly about changing into warm, dry clothes after getting dumped in the drink. Look for lightweight, waterproof, breathable synthetics, which take up minimal space. Supplex, Ultrasensor, and Solumbra clothes can be packed small but also provide UV protection.

Dry feet will make you much more comfortable. When your feet are damp and enclosed all day, athlete's foot is a distinct possibility. Be sure

A versatile headlamp is a must-have for nights outdoors. It can keep your hands free or convert to a flashlight, table light, clip-on safety light, or even a bike light. The Photon Freedom Fusion comes with dual beam colors with full-range adjustable brightness plus five safety beacons. (Photon Mico-light)

A durable, reliable light source is indispensable for performing camp chores such as cleaning a fish at night or washing dishes after dark. Many propane lanterns, such as the one pictured here, have a high-temperature globe that can stand up to long use and is also easily maintained. (The Coleman Company, Inc.)

▶ *Stiff uppers offer more ankle support when wading or portaging but are not as comfortable when kneeling.*
▶ *Knee-high rubber boots are ideal for entering and exiting the canoe without getting your feet wet.*

Cold, wet hands can mar an otherwise fun paddling trip. In moderate conditions, thin neoprene gloves are adequate; in colder weather, wear pogies—mittens that attach to the paddle while allowing your hands contact with the paddle shaft.

Do not scrimp on rain gear. The most serious problem you are likely to encounter while boat camping is hypothermia from chilly, rainy weather.

your feet are completely dry before going to bed. Some paddlers apply anti-athlete's foot powders or creams at the beginning of each paddling day. When shopping for paddling footgear, here are some things to keep in mind:

▶ *Sport sandals are light and airy. If they don't have loops over the big toes, you can wear them with neoprene socks in colder conditions.*
▶ *Soft-soled footwear flexes easily, which is ideal for kneeling in a canoe.*

PACKING

You'll enjoy your boat camping trip more if your gear is well organized and carefully packed. Certainly, you need to keep things dry. If your sleeping bag or food gets wet, you can kiss comfort good-bye. Even clothing can be difficult to dry when boat camping. You also want easy access to gear without having to pull every bag out of the kayak to inspect its contents to reach one item stashed in the bow.

Many different kinds of bags make for a good packing job:

Car Bag

Pack some fresh clothes and a towel for when you return to the car. Give a spare set of your car keys to one of your traveling companions. Chances are that both of you won't lose them.

Dry Bags

Even on the sunniest and warmest of days, some water will collect in the bottom of your boat, and you will be grateful for these bags. They're made of waterproof, abrasion-resistant fabric and have special watertight closures. The fabric is pliable enough to scrunch into whatever shape is needed.

Big, backpack-style dry bags are ideal for canoeists, especially when portaging. Big dry bags won't fit under most kayak decks, which are more conducive to several smaller bags. These can be stowed more compactly, with less wasted space. Big bags are ideal for protecting sleeping bags and clothing. They're impractical for packing small objects, because the one item you want is almost invariably at the bottom.

Tapered dry bags fit into the oddly shaped ends of kayak compartments with less wasted space. These are more expensive, for their size, than larger bags, but for serious kayak touring they are very useful.

Compression Bags

Small compression bags are like nylon stuff sacks with sturdy end caps connected by straps, which help compress your clothes or sleeping bag to about half the original size. Pack these inside a dry bag to help dry things stay that way.

Waterproof bags (dry bags) keep gear dry and safe even if you flip over. (Jonathan Hanson)

Bag for Day Gear

A medium-size bag or waterproof box can hold items you might want to use during the day on the water, such as lunch, a change of clothes for unforeseen changes in the weather, and a first-aid kit. This is in addition to the deck bag or thwart bag (see "Kayak Accessories" and "Canoe Accessories" earlier in this chapter), which are for quick access to small items.

Day Pack

Even though you may be traveling from camp to camp by boat, you'll probably take some short walks.

Dry bags can be used to make a big sleeping bag small enough to fit into a kayak or canoe and prevent it from getting wet. I recommend using a variety of bag sizes to fit different areas of your craft. SealLine's Dry Seal roll-down closure provides excellent waterproofing. (SealLine)

A day pack comes in handy for carrying necessary items, such as a water bottle, snacks, a light jacket, and sunscreen. It can also be helpful for toting water bottles between the water supply and your campsite if the distance is more than a few yards.

───────────■───────────

SAFETY GEAR

Appropriate safety equipment is vital. Wear your life jacket at all times. Also ensure that the bilge pump, a signaling device, and a throw bag/rope are within reach.

Life Jacket—PFDs are de rigeur for all boaters (most states require that you carry one PFD for each person aboard your boat). Aside from the law, PFDs are particularly important for kayakers and canoeists. They provide buoyancy and warmth in case you capsize, and give you time to collect your wits and resolve potentially hazardous situations. So resist the temptation to use your life jacket as seat padding and *put it on.*

The right fit is crucial for safety and comfort. If you buy a PFD that's too large, it won't hold your head up in the drink. If you get a small one, you're sure to be uncomfortable and you'll be reluctant to put in on. So choose a life jacket based on your chest measurements. Once you put it on, tighten all straps beginning with the waist belt. Any chafing at your arms and shoulders will significantly diminish the pleasure of your trip. Look for streamlined design and large armholes for optimal freedom of movement.

Many styles are available, but stick with US Coast Guard approved type 3 models with zip fronts. These models are regarded as more comfy and less bulky than other life jackets. My PFD has pockets which I find to be very convenient. It's great for keeping small safety gear, as well as tide tables and lip balm. It has mesh pockets that permit the water to drain out.

Emergency Gear—Safety gear such as whistle, flares, ocean tape, and mirror should be stored in a pocket on your life vest in case you are separated from your craft. A small bag of emergency gear should also be prepared, containing flashlight, lighter, emergency blanket, extra flares, etc.

Throw Rope and Throw Bag—A throw rope is an important piece of safety equipment. It should be at least 60 feet long and stuffed, not coiled inside the throw bag. While almost everyone wants to be a hero and rescue someone, few will learn the skills in advance. Knowing how to use a throw rope means being able to consistently throw the rope to and pull to shore a swimmer who is floating by 30 feet from you.

Boating Repair Gear—While you can't anticipate every problem, it's important to take along basic repair items such as bungee cord, duct tape, fast setting expoxy, hot glue stick, rope or deck line, screw driver, stainless steel nuts, bolts, rudder cable, and wrenches for nuts and bolts.

First-Aid Kit—You'd be surprised at the number of accidents that occur on shore rather than on the water. Caught up in the moment, people catch splinters and cut feet while loading and unloading boats on the shore. Don't let a lack of first aid supplies jeopardize your trip, make you uncomfortable, or put your health in peril. I recommend investing in individual first aid kits, so you can customize it for your personal needs such as your prescription medication. Adventure Medical Kits makes a "Paddler's Series" kit especially designed for kayaking, canoeing, and white-water rafting. It is waterproof and the components come in re-sealable plastic bags with insert cards which list the module contents. Whatever your choice, be sure it's adequate for the duration and remoteness of your trip.

───────────■───────────

TRANSPORTING THE BOAT

Carrying the boat on the car presents another challenge. It goes without saying that your boat goes on the car empty; lifting a loaded boat onto a roof rack stresses you and the boat. When you're on the

PACKING TIPS

An off-balance load, however slight, can compromise stability. Your gear should be distributed so the boat "trims" properly— level left to right and front to back. Keep the center of gravity as low as possible, and leave enough room for you and any passengers to sit and paddle comfortably. If your gear is piled higher than the gunwales, or is strapped to the deck of your kayak, you're packing too much.

Canoeists are at the greatest risk for losing gear in a capsize. To prevent this, you can either: a) lace a single line through the each pack's handle; or, b) use carabiners to attach the gear to a looped line. In either case, make sure the line is securely attached to a twart.

Kayakers stow their gear inside watertight hull compartments, so losing stuff isn't any issue for them. Reaching their gear within those compartments, on the other hand, can be difficult. Before packing small items into the narrow ends of the bow and stern, tie a light piece of line to them for future retrieval.

road, gear goes inside your vehicle or in a roof-rack-mounted gear box, not in the boat.

Yakima and Thule, the biggest makers of high-quality roof racks, have long sold special "saddles" that make fastening down canoes and kayaks much easier and more secure than just lashing them to bare crossbars. (There are different saddles for different-shape canoes and kayaks, and they can be easily removed and switched.)

Recently, things have gotten even better. Yakima now sells a special arm that telescopes out from the crossbars, so you don't have to lean over your vehicle to place the boat on top of it. This is especially useful on tall vehicles such as vans and SUVs. The Thule Hullavator is a kayak lift system that goes one step further; it eliminates the need to raise the boat to roof height in the first place. The boat cradles hinge from the rack down to about waist height. You position the boat in the cradles, and a gas-charged strut helps lift the boat onto the roof.

Here are a few ideas for transporting a canoe or kayak from the car to the water and back.

LEARN THE SKILLS

Before embarking on a boat camping adventure, you need to acquire adequate kayaking or canoeing skills to control your craft in wind and rough water. Otherwise, anxiety and discomfort will ride with you on your journey.

If you don't know any experienced paddlers to show you how it's done, search for a local paddling club near you. Check out local chapters of the Sierra Club (sierraclub.com) or the American Canoe Association (acanet.org). Some offer formal courses of instruction. You'll be in good company, and the cost is low. Another possibility is to check out a nearby college. Many offer noncredit canoeing and kayaking courses. You'll have to pay tuition, but they'll supply the equipment. If none of these leads work out, find a local outfitter who offers instruction.

OUTFITTERS

Professional outfitters can do a lot more than just provide a shuttle to make your trip more comfortable. Especially if your planned trip isn't close to home, you can rely on an outfitter to rent you canoes, kayaks, and camping gear, provide route-planning services (complete with maps), and supply you with a full gourmet menu, labeled and packed meal by meal for efficiency. Some will even handle transportation to and from the airport for you.

Got wheels? A lightweight boat cart provides a convenient method of portaging your kayak or canoe. (Doug Hayward)

The Hullavator is an elevator for your kayak. While it has the potential to lift canoes, the design has not yet been fine-tuned for that purpose. (Thule)

Two-wheeled carts are useful if your portage is over pavement, but they're a nuisance if it's through the woods. If you want to take the cart with you in your canoe or kayak, choose one that can be easily disassembled into smaller parts for easy stowage. The cart should also be relatively light (up to about 9 pounds) yet durable enough to handle tough trails.

CHAPTER 10

RVING

Ah, the irresistible call of the not-so-wild. If camping in a tent or sleeping on hard ground isn't your idea of a rewarding experience with nature, why not try a recreational vehicle (RV) vacation? It's your ticket to ride while bringing along all the comforts of home. Here you have transportation, kitchen, bedroom, and bath at your fingertips. At the same time, you simply turn on the ignition to see new sights and open yourself up to fresh adventures.

In an RV you are master of your universe. You can explore the country at your own pace or take off for last-minute mini-vacations. What's more, you are liberated from many of the hassles associated with travel: no hauling heavy bags in and out of costly hotel rooms; no need to rely on expensive or unhealthy restaurant food; no airplanes, trains, or buses to hurry up and wait for; and no tight schedules to follow.

RVs are the fastest-growing means of vacationing in the United States. One in twelve vehicle-owning families own an RV. A leading force behind RV ownership's upswing is the comfort-conscious baby boomer generation, although the biggest gains in RV ownership come from those under thirty-five.

An RV vacation at a campground is particularly attractive to families looking to rejuvenate ties with one another while they try new things. After a day of sightseeing, mom, dad, and the kids can return to their RV, cook a favorite meal at leisure, and bond in a comfortable and familiar atmosphere. An RV is also a boon to people with disabilities. Thousands of outdoor enthusiasts with special needs are recapturing their mobility and having more fun.

Some people are surprised to discover how much an RV opens up a new world of vacationing. Often it forces them to reconsider their prejudices about this mode of travel. Men who love being pampered in cushy hotels and have never camped except to bivouac in the army discover that they get a kick out of rolling around in a travel trailer or a motorhome and sleeping on the vehicle's innerspring mattress.

At the other end of the spectrum are rugged outdoor types such as backpackers and cyclists who

HISTORY OF THE RV

The combination of home and automobile for vacation purposes has been around for more than a century. The early adopters were traveling salesmen, gypsy peddlers, horse traders, fortune tellers, wandering musicians, circus performers, and other itinerant people. Soon mainstream vacationers started remodeling their cars for vacationing purposes. In 1916, a Midwestern farm couple built a sleeping compartment on top of an automobile chassis and toured the Rockies, carrying along hens for a supply of eggs.

RV living was also celebrated by Nobel Prize–winning author John Steinbeck in *Travels with Charley*, a memoir of his three-month tour of forty U.S. states in 1960. Steinbeck and his poodle camped out in a truck, on the back of which was mounted a cabin in which Steinbeck could sleep, cook, and work.

In 1964 Ken Kesey and his Merry Pranksters inspired the hippie movement by romping across the country in a psychedelic-painted school bus equipped with bunks and dining equipment. Their misadventures were chronicled by Tom Wolfe in *The Electric Kool-Aid Acid Test*.

Since then, recreational vehicles have become a ubiquitous feature of the American landscape.

---

consider it a point of honor never to set foot in a recreational vehicle. The big problem for these folks seems to be semantics. If you think "camping" means going spartan and uncomfortable and moving under your own steam, you'll certainly never accept RVing as a form of camping. That's OK. Don't call it camping; call it RVing, as most RVers do, and enjoy it as an alternate, comfortable style of vacation.

RVing is without a doubt the most expensive form of camping. You could easily spend as much on an RV as a modest house. Luckily, you don't have to buy an RV to go RVing; a number of rental companies can get you on the road without a heavy investment.

TYPES OF RVS

RVs range from a simple place for sleeping and eating to luxury lodges on wheels. They fall into two general categories: motorhomes, which combine the vehicle and living space in a single unit; and towables, which are pulled by a separate tow vehicle.

Today, there is an RV for every taste and budget. Prices range from about $3,500 for a folding camping trailer, to roughly $14,000 for an average roomy trailer, to $75,000 or more for a luxurious motorhome. And on it goes! A $300,000 motorhome might offer so-called basement storage, a washer and dryer, and even a hot tub. You could even splurge for a model with an exquisite circular staircase. The sky's the limit.

Class A Motorhomes

RVIA Class A motorhomes are well appointed and roomy. They usually have a kitchen, bathroom, entertainment center, and central heating and air-conditioning. Slide-out rooms give added living space. Depending on model and floor plan, Class A motorhomes can sleep up to eight. They're especially good for boondocking (see below). A small vehicle can be towed behind for short side trips once the motorhome is parked. Ongoing maintenance, large size, and high price are disadvantages. Class A motorhomes typically cost $58,000 to $400,000.

Class A motorhome. (RVIA)

Class C motorhome. (RVIA)

Class B Motorhomes

Class B motorhomes are often referred to as a camper vans. Although cramped compared to their big brothers, they offer maximum mobility (they can be driven just about anywhere you drive a car) and provide basic facilities such as cooking, refrigeration, toilet, folding bed, and sink. They sleep up to four people. Class B motorhomes typically cost $41,000 to $74,000.

Class C Motorhomes

Class C motorhomes aren't necessarily smaller than Class B. The difference is that the driving area is separate from the living quarters; the living area is installed on a conventional truck chassis and a has sleeping area over the cab called a cab-over. They often include cooking facilities, refrigerator, heat, sinks, and a toilet. They sleep up to eight. Class C motorhomes typically cost $48,000 to $140,000.

Class B motorhome. (RVIA)

Pop-up trailer. (RVIA)

Pop-Up Trailers

A pop-up trailer, also known as a folding trailer or tent trailer, is a lightweight towable that is collapsed during transit and storage. Pop-ups are lightweight with low profiles; even small cars can tow them. They sleep up to eight. Pop-ups lack conveniences found in other types of RVs, but they're much more affordable. Pop-ups typically cost $4,000 to $13,000.

Truck Campers

A truck camper has built-in jack stands that allow the unit to be loaded on and off a pickup truck with relative ease. In some ways, truck campers have the

Truck camper. (RVIA)

Fifth-wheel travel trailer. (RVIA)

best of both worlds: when the camper is on, they essentially have a Class C motorhome; when the camper is off, they have practical transportation for the daily commute. Kitchen and bathroom facilities are available on most models. They sleep up to six. Truck campers typically cost $4,000 to $26,000.

Fifth Wheel

A fifth wheel is a towable. Generally, a portion of a fifth wheel extends over the bed of the pickup truck that's hauling it, which allows for spacious two-level floor plans. Fifth wheels usually include cooking facilities, refrigeration, heating, and air-conditioning as well as a bathroom. Some have panoramic picture windows and several slide-outs. They sleep up to six. Fifth wheels typically cost $13,000 to $100,000.

Sport Utility RVs

A Sport Utility RV, or toy hauler, is a newer kind of RV design. These units have a kitchen and toilet, so you can camp in comfort, but they also have a loading ramp and docking bay that allows you to bring along a recreational vehicle such as a motorcycle or an ATV. Toy haulers are available as motorhomes and towables. They sleep up to eight. Sport Utility RVs typically cost $21,000 to $52,000.

Travel Trailers

Travel trailers are a hybrid between a fifth wheel and a pop-up. They have rigid sides and slide-out tent sections. They're affordable and come in a wide range of floor plans and sizes. Travel trailers typically cost $8,000 to $65,000.

RV RENTALS

If you have never RVed, it's probably not a good idea to get into the sport by buying one. It's an expensive experiment that you may not like. Start

Sport Utility RV. (RVIA)

Travel trailer.

DRIVING AN RV

Newbies often wonder whether they can handle driving an RV. The simple answer is yes. With a little practice and training, anyone can learn how to drive a motorhome or tow a trailer, and no special driver's license is required. Almost all motorhomes have an automatic transmission, power steering, and power brakes, so physical strength isn't an issue. Most RV rental companies offer test drives and tips to help inexperienced drivers feel comfortable behind the wheel.

In some cases, you don't even need to drive the rig. Some RV parks maintain "park RVs"—special RV units that are permanently parked, hooked up to utilities, and available for rent. They are usually shorter than full-size motorhomes but have all the amenities. From an environmental standpoint, this is a smart way to cut down on gas guzzling.

by renting, perhaps several times. Consider a purchase only if you're convinced that RVing is for you.

There are more than 400 national chain outlets that rent RVs, so chances are you'll find one close to home or an airport. Check the Yellow Pages under "Recreation Vehicle—Rentals" or check rvra.org, which lists more than 340 rental companies in the United States and Canada.

Most rental companies maintain fleets in a variety of sizes and styles, from pop-ups to motorhomes. The most popular RV rentals are comfortable, compact, and easy-to-drive Class C motorhomes. According to the Recreational Vehicle Industry Association, rental prices are based on three factors: season, region, and unit size. Depending on the season, motorhomes rent from $70 to $170 per day; truck campers and travel trailers average $50 to $120 per day. Weekly rates are lower.

Most RV rental agencies provide a "housekeeping" package that includes all the cookware and tableware you'll need to prepare food. The package is generally free, but you will be charged if pieces are missing when you return the unit, or if you bring the dishes back dirty. Most agencies require you to bring your own bed linens and will advise you of bed sizes in advance.

Once you've chosen your vacation destination, you can either rent an RV near your home and drive there, or fly to the location and rent an RV when you arrive. Many rental outlets at popular destinations offer special packages that bundle the RV rental with flight tickets.

Be sure to have your wits about you when the dealer hands you the rental agreement. You are contracting for the rental of an expensive piece of equipment. Find out if unlimited mileage is included or if you'll be charged for overage. If it's not included, what's the fee per mile? Rentals usually do not include fuel; be sure to factor this into your expense budget. Understand what insurance coverage is provided by the rental firm, the deductible limits for which you are responsible, and what you must pay to reduce your potential liability expense.

■

CAMPSITES

Making Reservations

Reservations at public and private campgrounds are desirable—if not essential—during peak season. When booking a campsite, ask about the proximity of your campsite to campground amenities. Do you want to be in a lakeside site? Near (or far from) the restrooms, activity hall, or swimming pool? In the thick of things, or out on the fringes? Make sure the site will accommodate your rig; some sites may be too short for a large towed vehicle or too narrow for your slide-outs. If backing up your rig is a hassle, ask for a pull-through campsite.

Parking

Sometimes it is clear how to orient the rig on a site; it may even have a cement parking pad. But in most cases, the only hint will be the hookup for electric, water, and sewer. Look at your neighbors and see how they're oriented—nose in or nose out, and at what angle. There is more space between rigs when everyone is roughly parallel to one another. In general, it's best to find a shady spot, which will make life more comfortable and save wear and tear on the air-conditioner.

Systems

As soon as your rig is positioned on the campsite, plug in the power cord and make sure the electricity works. Then unplug it and set about leveling your rig, following the instructions provided by the manufacturer or rental company. Then reattach the electricity, and hook up to the water and sewer. Now it's time to start making the campsite your own: roll out the awning, set out your patio furniture and barbecue, and relax.

BOONDOCKING

RVing is expensive. One way to cut costs is to avoid campgrounds. Camping for free and without utility hookups is called *boondocking*. Not only will you save money by boondocking, you may also enjoy a quieter camping experience, with greater solitude, and a closer proximity to nature—or not, as we'll see below.

RVers who frequently camp "off the grid" often equip their units with solar systems for electricity, but few rental RVs are set up for self-sufficiency. Nonetheless, boondocking still represents a viable option for one or two nights at a time. Just make sure that your water tanks are topped off, your house batteries are fully charged, and there's enough room in your holding tank. Then conserve your resources until you're ready to leave.

The term *boondocking* used to conjure up images of romance and adventure, the intrepid camper bivouacking in rough country. There are many official boondocking campsites in remote areas, such as on U.S. Forest Service or Bureau of Land Management land. More often, however, boondocking means camping under the beckoning blue glow of a Wal-Mart sign. Most Wal-Marts permit a free overnight stay in the parking lot. So do some casinos and other large commercial establishments. Some municipalities permit boondocking in public parks. Some malls and fraternal organizations such as the Elks Club may also allow boondocking. It's never okay to just assume that you're welcome, however. Always ask first.

If you find a spot where boondocking is permitted, you should know there's etiquette to observe. Just because you can camp overnight at a Wal-Mart or town park doesn't mean you can open the awnings, set up the grill, crack a beer, and loosen your belt. In these locations you're expected to live inside your unit, and not spread out as you would in a rented campsite.

There are numerous books available about free camping; an excellent one is *RV Boondocking Basics: A Guide to Living Without Hookups*. Also check out www.freecampgrounds.com and www.boondocking.org.

APPENDIX A

Camping Checklists

GENERAL CAMPING EQUIPMENT

Shelter/Bedding/Furniture

Camp chairs
Folding table
Groundsheet
Lantern
Pillows
Poles, stakes, and lines
Portable screen room
Rain fly
Seam sealer & Tent repair kit
Shade canopy/dining fly
Sleeping bag
Sleeping pad, air bed, or cot
Solar panel
Tent
Whisk broom and dustpan

Clothes

Bandanna
Belt
Clothesline and clothespins
Gloves/mittens
Hats/caps
Jacket
Pants
Poncho/raingear
Shirts
Shorts
Socks (hiking and regular)
Shoes, sandals, and hiking boots
Swimsuit
Underwear

Kitchen

Cleaning

Camp soap
Cleaning sponge
Dishpan
Dishtowels
Paper towels
Scrub pad
Table cloth
Trash bags
Wet wipes
Ziplock bags

Cooking

Aluminum foil
Bucket
Can opener
Charcoal
Coffee pot & filters
Cooler
Corkscrew
Cutting board

Stove/Campfire

Fire gloves
Fire starter
Fuel/fuel cartridge
Grill
Kindling
Lighter fluid
Matches and/or lighter
Reflector oven
Wood

Utensils

Bowls
Dutch oven
Knives, forks, spoons
Large food prep knives
Large serving spoon
Marshmallow forks
Measuring cup
Mixing bowl
Mugs, cups
Plastic wine glasses
Plates
Potholder
Pots and pans
Skillet
Stew pot
Strainer tongs
Veggie peeler

Water
Vacuum bottle/thermal jug
Water container (like collapsible
    water jugs)
Water-filtering pump
Water-purifying tablets

Tools
Flashlight or headlamp
Folding saw
Hatchet
Knife
Rope
Safety pins
Sewing kit

Toiletries
Comb/hair brush
Deodorant
Ditty sack (for dirty clothing)
Ear plugs
Glasses
Laundry detergent (biodegradable)
Razor
Shampoo
Soap (biodegradable)
Sunglasses
Toothbrush and toothpaste
Toilet paper
Washcloths

Health & Safety
First-Aid Kit
Adhesive bandages in a variety
    of sizes
Adhesive surgical tape
Ace bandage
Antibacterial cream
Antihistamine tablets or other
    allergy treatments
Antiseptic fluid (Dettol or
    Betadine)
Cold pack. For reducing swelling
    from bumps, bites, and minor
    burns
Disinfectant hand-cleaning gel
Eye drops
Gauze

Insect repellent with a high
    concentration of DEET
Iodine
Latex gloves
Lip balm with sunscreen
Liquid bandage (a paint-on liquid
    that dries but remains flexible
    to seal up minor cuts; especially
    useful on body parts that bend,
    such as fingers)
Liquid soap (useful for cleaning
    up scrapes)
Moistened towelettes
Nail clippers
Needle and thread
Nonprescription drugs (aspirin,
    acetaminophen, ibuprofen, or
    naproxen; anti-diarrheal;
    antacid; laxative)
Pain-relief ointment for insect
    stings and bites
Petroleum jelly or other lubricant
    (in tube)
Prescription medication in origi-
    nal containers
Safety pins
Sanitary napkins (two or three for
    very deep cuts)
Scissors
Sunscreen with SPF 30 +
Thermometer
Tongue depressors
Triangular bandages
Tweezers

Safety
Cellphone
List of important phone numbers
Signal mirror
Weather radio
Whistle

Activities
Backgammon
Bike/helmets
Binoculars
Books
Camera/film

Cards
Frisbee
Pad of paper/pencil/pen
Radio/CD/MP3 player
Sketch pad

Miscellaneous
Batteries
Daypack and/or fanny pack
Maps/brochures
Spare keys

BACKPACKING
See also General Camping Equip-
    ment beginning on page. 129

Backpack
Backpack cover
Backpacking stove with all
    accessories and parts
Backpacking tool kit (with
    Swiss army knife or multitool)
Compass
Eating and cooking utensils
    (Lexan or titanium for least
    weight)
Emergency blanket
Gaiters
GPS unit
Hiking boots or trail shoes
Hydration bladder or water
    bottles
Insect clothing
Sit pad
Stuff sacks for organizing gear
Trekking poles
Trowel
Waterproof breathable clothes
    based on layering system

BIKE CAMPING
See also General Camping Equip-
    ment beginning on page 129.
Basic bike tool kit
Bicycle (appropriate for touring)
Bike chain/lock
Camp/hiking shoes/sandals

Compass
Cycling shoes
Cycling shorts
Cycling socks
Daypack for side trips off the bike
Extra straps or bungee cords to
  secure gear
Flashing rear safety light
Front light with spare batteries
  and bulb
Handlebar bag
Helmet
Hydration bladder or two water
  bottles and carriers
One pair long pants
Padded cycling gloves
Patch kit
Rear and front racks and panniers,
  or trailer
Spare spokes (6+)
Spare tire
Spare tube
Tire pump/gage
T-shirts (cotton-synthetic blend)
Waterproofed maps
Wicking long-sleeve top
Wicking underwear
Windbreaker
Sunglasses

CANOEING AND KAYAKING

See also General Camping Equipment *beginning on page 129.*

Anchor and line
Basic kayak and canoe repair kit
Bilge pump
Bow and stern painters (rope)

Canoe or kayak
Chart case
Cockpit cover
Compass
Deck bags
Dry boxes
Dry bags
Duluth pack
Emergency marine flares
Eyeglass strap
Filet knife
Fishing rod and lures
Float bags
GPS unit
Ice chest
Large sponge
Mesh bags
Neoprene booties
Paddles (2 or 3)
Paddlefloat
Paddle leash
Paddling jacket
PFD (one for each person)
Plastic bailer
Plotter
Pogies or neoprene gloves
Quick-drying pants/shorts
Red flag (on back of transported
  boat)
Seat cushions and knee pads
Signaling devices
Sit pad or sleeping-pad chair kit
Spray skirt
Straps to tie in gear
Swimsuit
Tie-down line
Tide tables
Wading
Shoes/sandals/sneakers/hiking
  boots

Water bottles
Waterproof chart
Waterproof strobe
Waterproof watch
Wetsuit or drysuit

RVING

See also General Camping Equipment *beginning on page 129.*

All-purpose cleaner
Blocks of 2x lumber for leveling
  process
Bungie cords for strapping on
  equipment
Collapsible bicycle
Electrical tape
Emergency signaling devices
  (flashlight, flares, roadside
  emergency triangle markers,
  battery, red warning lights)
Fire extinguisher
Handheld vacuum cleaner
Laptop computer
Maps, atlas, travel guides
Plastic trashcans (one for galley,
  one for bath)
Portable fans
Portable generator (if dry camping
  anticipated)
Power adapters and extension
  cords
Roadside assistance information
RV operating manuals
Satellite or local TV
Set of tools for usual home repair
Smoke detector
Toilet paper (RV compatible)
VCR/DVD CD/ROM movies and
  games

APPENDIX B
Suppliers

ABO Gear (abogear.com)
Beach, outdoor, and pet products

Acorn (acorn.com)
Slipper socks, sandal socks, and other comfort
footwear

ACR Electronics (acrelectronics.com)
Outdoors and survival equipment

Adventure Foods (adventurefoods.com)
Instant food products for the outdoors

Adventure Medical Kits (adventuremedicalkits.com)
First aid kits for wilderness medicine, family outings,
travel, and sports emergencies

Air Grill (air-grill.com)
Tools to save time lighting fires, inflating rafts, and
cleaning grills

Alpine Aire Foods (alpineaire.com)
Emergency food and supplies for long-term survival,
preparedness, and self-sufficiency

Altrec (altrec.com)
Outdoor gear and apparel

Blue Ridge Chair Works (blueridgechair.com)
Portable outdoor furniture

Backpacker's Pantry (backpackerspantry.com)
Gourmet, freeze-dried backpacking food

Bell Canoe Works (bellcanoe.com)
Canoes and accessories for touring, recreational, and
family paddling

Bibler Tents (biblertents.com)
Single-wall tents for mountaineering and
backpacking

Big Agnes (bigagnes.com)
Sleeping bags, pads, and accessories

Black Diamond Equipment (blackdiamondequipment
.com)
Gear and apparel for climbing, skiing, and camping

Brunton (brunton.com)
Camping, GPS, and portable power equipment

Bushnell (bushnell.com)
Telescopes, binoculars, and weather-resistant
cameras

Buck Knives, Inc. (buckknives.com)
Knives for hunting, fishing, camping, hiking

Cache Lake (cachelake.com)
Dehydrated camping food

Camelbak (camelbak.com)
Hands-free hydration systems

Camping Logic (campinglogic.com)
Tent closets and gear lofts with lights

Camping Station
(campingstation.com)
Source for outdoor gear

Campmor, Inc. (campmor.com)
Camping, backpacking, hiking,
climbing, biking, and apparel

Cannondale Corporation
(cannondale.com)
Performance and recreational
bicycles, components and
accessories

Cabela's (cabelas.com)
Destination megastore that
sells hunting, fishing, and
outdoor gear

Cascade Designs
(cascadedesigns.com)
Manufacturers of technically
advanced outdoor
equipment

Chaco (chaco.com)
Boots and sport sandals

Coastline Adventures (coastlineadventures.com)
Outdoor gear and camping
equipment

Coleman (coleman.com)
Maker of lanterns, camp stoves,
coolers, tents, sleeping bags,
camp furniture, and related
camping and outdoor recreation equipment

Columbia Sportswear
(columbia.com)
Active outdoor apparel, skiwear,
and footwear

Cocoon Travel Gear
(designsalt.com)
Lightweight sleep gear for
travelers and backpackers

Crazy Creek Products
(crazycreek.com)
Portable lightweight outdoor
seating

Croakies (croakies.com)
Eyewear retainers, belts, watchbands, and other accessories.

Dagger Canoe (dagger.com)
Whitewater, touring, and recreational kayaks

Duofold (duofold.com)
Thermal underwear base-layer
apparel

Eagle Creek (eaglecreek.com)
Travel gear, luggage, travel accessories and packing aids

Eastern Mountain Sports
(EMS.com)
Outdoor gear and outdoor clothing for the active outdoor
enthusiast

Essential Gear
(essentialgear.com)
Distributors of high-tech survival
tools

Folbot, Inc. (folbot.com)
Manufacturer of folding kayaks

Garmin International
(garmin.com)
Navigation and communications
equipment

Granite Gear (granitegear.com)
Makers of backpacks, dog packs,
compression sacks, and canoe
gear

Gregory Mountain Products
(gregorypacks.com)
Expedition and backpacking
packs

GSI Outdoors (gsioutdoors.com)
Unique cookware and camp
furniture

Hardigg Industries (hardigg.com)
Rugged plastic protective cases

Helly Hansen (hellyhansen.com)
Protective technical gear for
sport, survival, and work

High Gear Radio (highgear.com)
High-performance tools that make
outdoor adventure fun and safe

Hilleberg (hilleberg.com)
Backpacking and mountaineering
tents

JanSport (jansport.com)
Sporting, hiking, traveling, and
business bags

Kelty, Inc. (kelty.com)
Tents, backpacks, and sleeping
bags.

Kokatat (kokatat.com)
Personal flotation, drysuits, insulation, and other clothing for
paddlers

Lafuma U.S.A. (lafumausa.com)
Outdoor furniture including
chairs and recliners

Life-Link (life-link.com)
Trekking poles for backcountry,
skiing, and expedition use

L.L. Bean, Inc. (llbean.com)
Destination megastore for clothing and outdoor equipment

Mad River Canoe
(madrivercanoe.com)
High-end canoes made from synthetic materials, including
Royalex and Kevlar

Mongoose (mongoose.com)
Purveyor of performance mountain, BMX, youth, and road bicycles

Mountainsmith
(mountainsmith.com)
Backpacks and outdoor sports gear

Marmot (marmot.com)
Packs, tents, sleeping bags, and outdoor clothing

Merrell Footwear
(merrellboot.com)
Performance footwear, packs, and bags

MSR (Mountain Safety Research) (msrcorp.com)
Tents, stoves, cookware, and water treatments

Nalgene (nalgene-outdoor.com)
High-quality plastic water bottles

Old Town Canoe and Kayak
(oldtowncanoe.com)
Canoes, kayaks, and accessories

Ortlieb USA (ortliebusa.com)
Panniers, backpacks, dry bags, water transport, and map cases

Outdoor Research (orgear.com)
Outdoor gear designed for adventure

Paha Que Wilderness, Inc.
(pahaque.com)
High-quality family camping tents

Panoptx (panoptx.com)
Eyewear for use in a variety of sports

Patagonia (patagonia.com)
Outdoor clothing and technical apparel

PhotonLight
(photonlight.com)
Flashlights and headlamps

REI/Recreation Equipment, Inc.
(rei.com)
Outdoor gear store

Royal Robbins
(royalrobbins.com)
Outdoor and travel clothing

Ruff Wear (ruffwear.com)
Gear for dogs with active lifestyles

Sea Eagle (seaeagle.com)
Inflatable kayaks and boats

SealLine (seallinegear.com)
Dry bags and rudder systems for water sports

Seattle Sports
(seattlesportsco.com)
Dry bags, travel, and adventure gear

Sierra Designs
(sierradesigns.com)
Camping and hiking gear

Slumberjack (slumberjack.com)
Sleeping bags, mats, and other outdoor furniture

Smart Wool (smartwool.com)
Socks, apparel, and accessories for outdoor activities

Steripen (hydro-photon.com)
Portable water purifier

Surefire (surefire.com)
Compact, high-intensity flashlights

Teva (teva.com)
Rugged sandals, hiking shoes, and all-terrain footwear

Therm-a-Rest (thermarest.com)
Self-inflating mattress, and closed-cell camping mattresses

The North Face
(thenorthface.com)
Makers of expedition tents, packs, shoes, sleeping bags, and apparel

Thor-Lo (thorlo.com)
Socks for camping, hiking, and other sports

Thule (thuleracks.com)
Car rack systems, bike carriers, roof boxes, ski carriers, and water sport carriers.

Timberland (timberland.com)
Outdoor wear, primarily boots

Timex (timex.com)
Watches, clocks, eyewear, pedometers, and weather instruments

Tough Traveler
(toughtraveler.com)
Baby carriers, luggage, and backpacks

Tula Hats (tulahats.com)
Hats for outdoor enthusiasts, travelers, and adventurers

Victorinox Swiss Army
(swissarmy.com)
Apparel, travel gear, timepieces, cutlery, and multi-tools

Voltaic (voltaicsystems.com)
Backpacks designed as power generators to charge devices while traveling

W.L. Gore & Associates, Inc.
(gore.com)
Materials and technology for
outerwear comfort, and
protection

Woolrich (woolrich.com)
Outdoor clothing and sporting
accessories

Yakima Products
(Yakima.com)
Racks for bikes, boats, ski
equipment, and gear

APPENDIX C
Resources

Organizations

American Canoe Association (ACA) (acanet.org)
Promotes canoeing, kayaking, rafting, and river conservation.

Adventure Cycling Association (adv-cycling.org)
Bicycle travel inspiration and resource.

American Alpine Club (americanalpineclub.org)
Mountaineering and climbing.

American Hiking Society (americanhiking.org)
Dedicated to serving hikers and protecting hiking trails.

Appalachian Mountain Club (outdoors.org)
Nation's oldest outdoor recreation, education, and conservation organization.

Appalachian Trail Conference (appalachiantrail.org)
Volunteers and club affiliates protect and maintain the Appalachian Trail.

Bureau of Land Management (BLM) (blm.gov)
Agency administers 258 million surface acres of America's public lands, located primarily in 12 Western States.

Family Campers & RVers Association FCRV (fcrv.org)
Organization dedicated to camping fellowship.

Hostelling International USA (hiusa.org)
Network of budget hostel accommodations.

National Outdoor Leadership School (nols.edu)
Wilderness education school offering expedition length courses in eight countries.

National Park Service (nps.gov)
Federal agency that manages all National Parks.

National Wildlife Federation (NWF) (nwf.org)
Organization to protect wildlife.

Nature Conservancy (nature.org)
Organization dedicated to protecting land and water for nature and people.

North American Family Campers Association (nafca.org)
All volunteer organization for people who enjoy camping with family.

Outdoor Explorations (outdoorexplorations.org)
Adventure programs, training, and community service for people with disabilities.

Outward Bound (outwardbound.org)
Offers opportunities for experiential learning and personal growth through adventure-based wilderness programs.

Recreation Vehicle Industry Association (rvda.org)
National association dedicated to advancing the RV retailers interests.

Recreation Vehicle Rental Association (rvra.org)
A national association of dealers who rent recreational vehicles.

Sierra Club (sierraclub.org)
Organization to preserve wildlands, save endangered and threatened wildlife, and protect the environment.

Wilderness Society (wilderness.org)
Protects and conserves America's wilderness and roadless areas.

U.S. Army Corps of Engineers (CorpsLakes.us)
The Nation's largest provider of outdoor recreation.

USA Cycling (usacycling.org)
Family of organizations that promote and govern different disciplines of cycling.

United States Canoe Association (uscanoe.com)
Canoe and kayak group encouraging the growth of recreational, competitive, and racing paddling.

U.S. Fish and Wildlife Service (fws.gov)
Federal agency working to conserve, protect and enhance fish, wildlife, and plants and their habitats.

U.S. Forest Service (fs.fed.us)
Manages public lands in national forests and grasslands.

Magazines

Backpacker (backpacker.com)
Articles, gear reviews and destinations for backpacking, camping, hiking, and other outdoor activities.

Bicycle (bicycling.com)
Publication devoted to road biking, mountain biking, and cycling.

Camping Life (campinglife.com)
Articles about interesting destinations, products, and activities for family campers.

Canoe & Kayak (canoekayak.com)
Canoeing and kayaking techniques, and paddling gear reviews.

Outside (outside.away.com)
Active lifestyle and adventure-travel magazine.

Paddler (paddlermagazine.com)
Articles and stories on places to canoe and kayak as well as gear reviews and profiles.

INTERNET RESOURCES

Backpacker.com
Hiking, backpacking, camping, and outdoor wilderness travel website from *Backpacker* magazine.

CampUSA.com
Directory of campgrounds in the United States.

Cruiseamerica.com
RV rental and sales stores with over 160 locations in the United States and Canada.

eBay.com
Broker site to buy and sell electronics, camping gear, sporting goods, cars, clothing, apparel, collectibles, and everything else.

Craigslist.com
Forums for sale of goods including camping gear as well as jobs, housing, personals, and community events.

Geartrade.com
Used and new gear broker/site that lets sellers and specialty retailers set their own prices.

gorp.away.com
Resource for adventure travel and outdoor recreation.

Ownersrental.com
RV and motorhome rentals by owner.

Reserveamerica.com
Comprehensive directory of campsites in the United States.

FAMILY CAMPING

Asbury Hills Camp and Retreat Center, Cleveland, SC (asburyhills.org)

Blue Star Camps, Hendersonville, NC (bluestarcamps.com)

Camp Alleghany, Lewisburg, WV (campalleghany.com)

Camp Luther, Lake Erie, OH (lomocamps.org)

Camp Nebagamon, Lake Nebagamon, WI (campnebagamon.com)

Cazadero Performing Arts Camp, Cazadero, CA (cazadero.org)

Colorado Heritage Camps, CO
(9 in Rockies, 1 in Denver)
(heritagecamps.org)

Farm & Wilderness Camp,
Plymouth, VT (fandw.org)

Pine Cove, The Bluffs and the
Woods, Tyler, TX
(pinecove.com)

Star Island, Portsmouth, NH
(starisland.org)

**Western Unitarian Universalist
Life Festival**, Ghost Ranch,
NM (wuulf.org)

Wyonegonic, Denmark, ME
(wyonegonic.com)

YMCA Camp Pendalouan,
Montague, MI
(pendalouan.org)

GUIDED TRIPS AND SOCIAL EVENTS

Alaska Alpine Adventures
(alaskaalpineadventures
.com)
Custom, personalized, and gourmet small-group adventures
throughout Alaska's national
parks and wildlife refuges.
Hiking, backpacking, rafting,
kayaking, mountaineering, and
more.

American Alpine Institute
(mtnguide.com)
Climbing school and guide service
specializing in basic, intermedi-
ate, and advanced training and
expeditions. Offers courses,
climbing trips, and expeditions
in WA, CA, CO, AK, and NV
as well as abroad.

Appalachian Mountain Club
(outdoors.org)
Founded in 1876, the AMC hosts
thousands of outdoor recreation
activities per year, including
hiking, biking, canoeing,
kayaking, climbing, and skiing,
as well as social events.

Arnott's Lodge & Hiking
(arnottslodge.com)
Hawaiian hostel offering outings
to volcanoes, waterfalls, and
beaches for snorkeling.

Big Wild Adventures
(bigwildadventures.com)
Guided hiking trips exploring the
Rocky Mountains of Wyoming
and Montana. Other trips
take campers into the canyons
and highlands of Arizona,
New Mexico, and southern
Utah.

Call of the Wild (callwild.com)
Women's adventure travel company offering beginning and

challenging backpacking trips
in the wilderness.

Leave No Trace Adventures
(leavenotrace.com)
Introduction to backpacking, hiking, and environmental awareness.

Outward Bound
(outwardbound.com)
Outdoor leadership program providing trips geared to develop-
ing wilderness skills, teamwork,
and confidence.

**Rendezvous Backcountry
Adventures**
(hikethetetons.com)
Wyoming guide service offering
backpacking, skiing, and snow-
boarding trips in the Teton
Mountains.

Sky Island Treks
(skyislandtreks.com)
Guided backpacking trips in
Grand Canyon and Saguaro
national parks on established
trails as well as remote corners
of the canyon.

**Yellowstone Backpacking
Custom and Family Trips**
(bigwildadventures.com)
Builds trips around your personal
or group interests to remote
corners of North America.

Index

Numbers in **bold** indicate pages with illustrations